THE NATURALIST'S HANDBOOK

(Previously entitled *The Junior Naturalist's Handbook*)

Geoffrey G. Watson is Curator of the Teesside
Museum and Art Gallery Department,
Chairman-Director of Yorkshire Field
Studies, and Founder-Director of the British
Young Naturalists' Association.

THE NATURALIST'S HANDBOOK

(Previously entitled *The Junior Naturalist's Handbook*)

GEOFFREY G. WATSON

Cover illustration by David Pratt
Text illustrations by Mary Storry and
Robin Lawrie

A Piccolo Book

PAN BOOKS LTD : LONDON

First published 1962 as *The Junior Naturalist's Handbook*
by Adam and Charles Black Ltd
This edition published 1973 by Pan Books Ltd,
33 Tothill Street, London SW1

ISBN 0 330 23585 0

© Geoffrey G. Watson 1962

To Nicholas

Made and printed in Great Britain by
Cox & Wyman Ltd, London, Reading and Fakenham

CONTENTS

AUTHOR'S PREFACE

This book owes its origin to Edith, Jean, Hilary, Alan, David, John, Howard, Peter, Judith and Derek who shared many expeditions and adventures with me in search of specimens, and whose friendship I shall always value. It is, I hope, the Handbook the original ten always wished for and fulfils the requirements they stipulated in our many discussions on such a book.

I am indebted to many people, particularly the Libraries Committee and my Director, Mervyn Edwards, MA, FLA, for their continued interest in my work with young people. To Dr R. Pickering, FGS, who read the original typescript and made many valuable suggestions and to Mrs A. Tyman who gave unsparingly of her time to type the manuscript.

I am grateful to Harry Scott for allowing me to use a number of articles previously published in *Young Naturalist*.

PART ONE

1 COMFORT OUTDOORS

Comfort outdoors can mean the difference between enjoyment and misery, and perhaps even between health and illness. Comfort does not come from modish and expensive equipment, but from following the practice and benefiting from the experience of many explorer-naturalists and backwoodsmen, who had to learn the hard way.

Comfort is particularly important, whether you are walking one mile or ten miles, because if you are not comfortable your enthusiasm will be lost before the real pleasures and delights of discovery are realized. The touchstone of true outdoor comfort is serviceable clothing, selected to help the body maintain its normal temperature in heat, rain, frost or wind. The emphasis is on help as the body should be encouraged to do its share.

Perspiration is the heat-regulating mechanism of the body, and you should select suitable clothes which will not hinder its passage from the skin. For this reason alone, it is important that all clothing is permeable to air, so that the body can breathe. In summer, perspiration forms very rapidly and evaporates off the body: clothing in this case should be light, from head to toe, and exceptionally permeable. In winter, protection is needed against the cold; this must not come from wearing many layers of underclothes next to the skin but from adding extra outer (permeable) garments to protect the body against the cold and prevent the too rapid cooling of the body temperature.

One of the easiest ways of catching a serious chill is to wear clothing that does not permit the passage of air. The discomfort of rubber capes, oilskins, wellingtons, overshoes and waders are proof enough. Wellingtons, even when worn with thick woollen stockings to absorb the perspiration, cause tired and aching feet even in the coldest weather.

Clothing

Tight clothing is another fetish of town wear and really is an abomination you must avoid, as it will interfere with circulation. Any restriction to the body should be avoided wherever possible, as it can cause additional perspiration and irritation, and give the muscles much more work to do.

Underclothing is important too, and should have your first consideration. It must be loosely woven to absorb moisture and to allow warm pockets of air to form in the weave of the material. These act as air conductors, saving the body from sudden changes of temperature.

Woollen or flannel shirts of the army pattern are useful. They have the advantage of an attached collar, while certain styles have pockets which are useful to hold odds and ends of personal equipment.

Trousers should be durable, preferably of a material which does not tear easily. Corduroy tears easily, while woollen trousers pick up burrs and catch in bracken or coarse grass. Again, army pattern trousers are both cheap and strong; if you wear them with a belt, have it as loose as you can.

An anorak with hood and pockets will complete your out-door clothes. Never tie it round your middle, rather let it flap.

The selection of footwear should rate high in the consideration of your outdoor comfort. You will find there is nothing worse than aching or blistered feet; one or other can make a nightmare of any expedition. Shoes are never really very satisfactory over rough country, as they afford very little protection to the foot or ankle, and how easily the ankle can turn on stony or uneven ground. Boots are most suitable, provided they do not come too high up on the ankle. They need to be high enough to give support, but not so high as to exclude air. Good leather allows the passage of air and the foot can breathe provided the pores are not clogged with polish. Stockings, not socks, should be worn and should be made of soft wool as they help to ventilate the boot.

The Junior Naturalist ready to go

Care of the feet

'An ounce of prevention is worth a pound of cure.'

Feet can be toughened or hardened before starting on a hike by soaking them the night before in a solution of alcohol and salt, or in one made by dissolving a teaspoonful of tannic acid in a wash bowl of cold water. A little alum in water may be substituted.

Every morning, before starting on a hike, rub some

French chalk or talc over the feet and dust some inside your boots. If you have no French chalk or talc, rub with vaseline or melted tallow. Soap is often used for the purpose, but some soaps contain too much free alkali which is bad for the feet.

The main thing is to keep the feet clean. Wash them well every evening, preferably in hot salted water. If they are strained or swollen massage them while bathing. The nails should be cut short and square. If you suffer from an ingrowing toe-nail, a small V cut in the nail will eliminate this trouble. If the feet are washed during the day this should be done briskly, and not by soaking, otherwise they will be tender.

Should you step in water over your boot-tops, or get your feet wet in any other way, stop as soon as you can and wring out your stockings; do not walk them dry, for this makes the skin tender.

Thick woollen stockings help to ventilate the feet in the following way. When your weight is thrown on one foot, as in stepping forward, the air that was confined in the meshes of the fabric is forced out to the top of the boot; then, when the pressure is released, fresh air is sucked back to fill the partial vacuum.

Thin socks, particularly cotton ones, become saturated with perspiration and little or no air can get into them. The feet then have their pores clogged and become tender. Thin stockings also admit sand and dirt more quickly than thick ones.

Blisters should be treated immediately by pricking with a sterilized needle. Gently press out the fluid and apply a dressing, fastened with adhesive plaster. If not treated immediately, the blister will burst, stick to the stocking and possibly get infected.

Care of the feet is important, as is the careful dressing of your feet in the morning. The time taken is well worth the trouble, and will save a great deal of inconvenience and time wasted in adjusting your stockings on the journey.

Two pairs of soft woollen stockings should always be

worn with boots, and both pairs freely dusted with French chalk or talcum before they are put on. This prevents the rubbing or knotting of the stockings, thus eliminating the cause of blisters.

The top pair of stockings should be turned down over the boot tops to prevent grit or pebbles getting in. The second pair should be turned up over your trousers to stop them flapping. Loose trousers are a nuisance, particularly when going through thick vegetation.

On long journeys, stockings should always be changed at midday.

Walking is in itself quite an art, particularly the stride which is both comfortable and noiseless – both necessary factors when searching for wild life in woodland. The Red Indian, for example, moves gracefully, though his walk has a slight rolling motion caused by putting his foot flat on the ground and rolling his body slightly at the same time. This is something you might well try. Point your left foot directly forward or slightly inward, so that the weight of your body is equally distributed from your toes through to the ball of your foot and to your heels; at the same time sway your left hip one inch or so slightly to the side. Repeat this for the right foot, then left foot again and so on, and you will find you have perfect balance. This walk is also typical of sailors, who can move with complete ease and balance even in the roughest seas. By walking in this way your foot comes to feel the ground before the weight of the body is placed upon it, leaving your eyes free to cover the ground in front of you. Town folk walk on their toes; which, although it might look very nice and gives a springy athletic step, can be dangerous.

The knee action should be loose and springy, particularly when going uphill, and the pace should be regulated and rhythmic, thus giving tireless, sure-footed progress.

Never exhaust yourself; keep a steady pace and stop whenever you feel the pull and your breathing is laboured. A stop should never be for more than five minutes, otherwise your muscles will stiffen up and your body will chill. Go steadily and let the others do the showing-off.

Remember – if you are limping it is impossible to hurry after a rare or unusual butterfly, nor can you crawl several yards to see fox cubs playing outside their earth if you are wearing your best suit. Benefit from experience, dress yourself comfortably and every expedition, whatever the weather, will be a lasting pleasure.

2 THE YOUNG NATURALIST

The first step to becoming a good field naturalist is to know your district thoroughly, and this can best be done by buying a one-inch-to-the-mile Ordnance Survey map; study it carefully and visit each part of your area, using your map as a guide. You will be surprised at the countryside which you never realized existed within a few miles of your home. More important still, you will gradually realize the varied type and character of the countryside – woodland, moor, bog and river, each with its own distinct fauna and flora.

Maps not only become old friends, but can be regarded as reference works of journeys taken and finds made. Using your own abbreviations, you can mark – very carefully, of course, otherwise you will obliterate the conventional signs – the site of your discoveries. An old but very well-used map in my possession marks all the known badger sets and fox earths in an area covering ten square miles – a very useful reference, better than many pages of notes.

Using a map in this way not only gives you a 'feel' of the countryside, but also takes you down little-known country lanes, bridle paths and through farmyards into remote corners of your area among the country people. These are cautious folk, wary of strangers, yet often possessing a wealth of nature lore. You can win their respect and trust by considerate behaviour out-of-doors. Show that you not only know the country code, but practise it. Damage to property, crops or farm animals can be done unwittingly; boys with an untrained dog crossing pasture during lambing time can cause intense suffering; climbing a gate by the latch weakens if not breaks the gate; striding over dry-stone walls can bring them down. Thoughtless behaviour of this sort will anger a farmer, and he will lose all sympathy, not only with the young naturalist but also with many other outdoor people, such as ramblers.

When you find you have to cross some fields to a fox earth or badger set, or if you wish to explore a copse, go to the farm and explain to the farmer that you are interested in wild life, what particular animal or plants you are looking for, and ask his permission to cross fields. In return for his kindness you can offer your services at hay-making or harvest time, and this would be very greatly appreciated. Farmers, keepers, even poachers have a tremendous practical knowledge of wild life, based on many years of observation in the field. This information is invaluable, particularly as it may include observations of animal behaviour not previously witnessed by naturalists nor to be found in any book.

Books

Every young naturalist should have a small library of well-chosen books on natural history for reference purposes. Books, however, must never become an end in themselves. The true naturalist, the field naturalist, is an outdoor man using his eyes, ears and nose as his guide to the living world, and not a book-worm.

Like human beings, animals are individualists, and their behaviour and habits are unpredictable. A book will give you an animal's name, it will describe its colour and shape, where it lives, when its young are born – but its behaviour will only be briefly sketched, except in rare instances. Think back to your last field trip, and try to remember, if you have not got your field note-book handy, whether the behaviour of the chaffinch you saw was the same as that of the chaffinch that lives at the bottom of your garden. The rookery is an ideal place to study individuality. No book can portray the personality of animals; it is something which can only be glimpsed and enjoyed by constant field work.

For leisure reading, borrow from your local library books written by the famous explorer-naturalists. Some of these give adventure at its best; remember, they were written by naturalists who had no reference library to help them, but had to verify their facts by observation, investigation and experiment.

Museums and natural history societies

A visit to a natural history museum will be of enormous help. In the public galleries you will see mounted specimens of most of the birds and mammals that occur in your area. These you can study at leisure and compare with the illustrations and descriptions in your handbook. Speedy recognition of field characters is most important outdoors; this is particularly necessary when birds flash past in flight. Points for recognition are most easily learned by examining, preferably in the hand, mounted birds or cabinet skins.

Many museums possess collections of flowers, birds, mammals, shells and insects. These collections, beautifully kept, systematically arranged and frequently added to, are available for use by students. If there is any specimen you would particularly like to see, and it does not appear on display in your local museum, ask to see the keeper or curator, and he will be only too delighted to take you through the study rooms to give you the opportunity of seeing the specimen. Later perhaps you may get the opportunity of working with the study material, and accompanying members of the museum staff on expeditions to collect in the field.

Many towns have their natural history society, whose members have spent years studying the wild life of their district and have amassed tremendous knowledge of the sites of many of the locally found species. Sometimes these are listed in printed catalogues or books, which can be bought; otherwise they are entered in record books in the possession of society members who are known as recorders. The names of the recorders are usually listed on the syllabus or club membership card of the society. As you enter into natural history circles you will find someone who will introduce you to the secretary of your local society, who in turn will give you full details of membership and put your name forward if you are thought to be a right and proper person to become a member of that society.

Equipment

The chapters in Part II of this guide list the basic equipment necessary to collect in the field. In every instance this equipment can be packed into a small space, such as a haversack, and is light and easy to carry.

Expeditions into the field can be divided into two forms. The first consists of exploration, when you carry your binoculars and field note-book. This is primarily a recording expedition to find out the types of animals that live in the habitat you are going to investigate and collect from in the future. The second form of expedition is to collect or observe, when your activities are restricted to working in one group. Remember, it is impossible to collect insects, watch birds, study a badger set and make plaster casts of spoor, and collect wild flowers all at the same time. If you tried, you would look like a Christmas tree, with your two haversacks, vasculum and binoculars – not to mention your camera and hide frame. To attempt to do too much means that you will miss a great deal in the field. Although you are restricting your activities, this in itself does not mean that you need not record other things you see. If you are collecting beetles, you might record in your field note-book the plants and the trees that you see in the vicinity; or the birds that are active round about you.

One of the best forms of haversack, which can be obtained from ex-army stocks, is the leather case used by dispatch riders during the last war. These cases are strongly made, are of suitable size and have buckles on either end for the attachment of a strap to put over your shoulder. A haversack of this sort, squared with hardboard, can have fitments arranged for your collecting equipment.

Collecting

The experienced naturalist always collects with discrimination. He knows the specimens that he requires, and he goes to the most likely locality where they can be obtained. Never collect more specimens than you need; some naturalists have made a practice of collecting dozens of insects at a time, taking them home, then killing them all and sorting out only the best to add to their collection, the rest being thrown away. There is no reason why you should not collect a number in the field, carefully examine them, and then release the ones which are not satisfactory for your purpose. With rare animals or plants you must be prepared to record only, putting the details in your field note-book. Never under any circumstances take a plant or animal that you know to be extremely localized in its distribution, or rare.

Care in collecting should be as much a part of the young naturalist's code as is his behaviour out-of-doors. Not only must you learn to collect discriminately and carefully, but you must at the same time attempt to stop anyone you see taking more than they need of any plant or animal group. All too often masses of bluebells or primroses are picked, and the collector tires before getting them home and throws them on the roadside. Plants and animals are living things, with lives that are as well regulated as our own. We observe them to record their behaviour, and we collect them to build up small study collections or to find out their names. If we collect for the latter purpose, then we must make sure that we take only what we require, and that living creatures are killed in a manner stipulated in this book, efficiently and painlessly.

If you keep animals under observation – such as snakes or frogs and toads in a vivarium, ants in a formicarium, snails or fish in an aquarium, or mammals in cages – then you must make sure that they are well looked after, and have sufficient room to move and food to eat.

Such mammals and birds as are added to your collection must only be those that are found dead. On no account must you use an airgun or a catapult to collect specimens. The young naturalist who did so could very easily find himself in a court of law, and be very severely fined. Regard all birds and mammals as protected, and make it a rule to collect only those you find dead, either killed by traffic or having died through natural causes.

3 TRAILS, TRACKS AND SIGNS

The excitement and thrill of the trail lie in watching and observing wild life, without yourself being seen. To do this successfully means that you should become experienced in woodcraft. This is not really as difficult as it sounds, provided you set out to learn the ways of nature and to understand the lore of the trail – the signs and clues of the animals which abound in our countryside.

A naturalist experienced in the art of woodcraft can make himself disappear by means of skilful camouflage. The clothes we wear should not contrast with the colours of nature, but be similar to them. Greens, greys and browns, provided they are not too light, all are colours that will blend with our woodland scenery. It is possible to go a step further and copy the leopard in our attempts to camouflage ourselves – not by painting spots all over our clothes, but by varying the colour of our jerkin, jeans and shirt. This helps to break up the shape of our bodies and we begin to merge into our background.

In our wandering along the trails which pass through our own countryside we shall see the signs of many birds and beasts, but rarely sight the animals. This is because animals are readily aware of danger through their acute sense either of smell or sight. The three signs which 'give away' the junior naturalist in the country are smell, movement and sound. Let us examine them in that order.

Smell

Most mammals have a strongly developed sense of smell and rely on this to warn them of danger. Wherever the young naturalist goes he will leave a scent track – minute droplets of his own scent which are carried by the wind. It is when an animal catches this wind-carried scent that it will bolt for cover.

Knowing this, the young naturalist should always make sure he approaches the animals he is going to study, either 'up-wind' or 'cross-wind', in such a way that the wind blowing towards the animal is free, or partially free, from human scent. You can test the wind by wetting your finger or by throwing some dust into the air. Even the lightest breeze can be found in one or other of these ways. You will only be successful in your stalking if the wind is blowing in your face as you crawl along the ground towards the animal.

'Cross-wind' is a term used in deer-stalking. When a herd of deer is resting on a hillside the stags conceal themselves at the foot of the hill with the hinds lying between them and the hill-top. The herd will be on the lee side of the hill so that it is sheltered from the wind. In this position it is very difficult to stalk the animals without either being seen by the stags as you approach up the valley or, on the other hand, your scent being carried down to them if you approach from above. There is only one method of stalking animals in this position, that is, to approach diagonally down the valley or 'cross-wind'.

Movement

Once an animal senses danger it 'freezes', then bolts for cover. Woodsmen, stalkers and scouts imitate animals when they are hunting. They always walk slowly and stealthily, or, if they are moving up-wind or cross-wind on deer, they

Top: Stalking, with the wind blowing your scent *away* from the animal
Middle: Crawling with the minimum of movement
Bottom: Sitting and watching

crawl silently inch by inch towards the herd. If they think the animal has got their scent they 'freeze' until it looks away or goes on feeding before they move again. A sharp movement will readily spell danger to most mammals and birds, and they will immediately bolt for cover.

There are ways of walking and crawling which you might like to practise. Start by walking very slowly, placing the whole of the flat of the foot on the ground. When you are successful try it again, but this time raise the knee three inches higher than you did before. Practise this until you do it automatically. If you walk on your toes you tend to lose your balance, but if you put the whole of your foot slowly down on the ground, with the feet pointing straight forward or inward, you will feel the twig or stone before you put your full weight on it. Lifting your knee three inches higher will save your feet from brushing through the grass or stumbling over a root.

To crawl, lie flat on the ground with your elbows bent and your hands flat on the ground just by your face. Bend your left knee, bringing it forward until it is level with your waist. Steady yourself, then press forward with your knee and elbows. Rest for a second or so before bringing your right knee up to the level of your waist and moving your hands back just by your face, before you move again. Using this method you will be able to crawl quickly and silently towards the animal you are watching.

As you become practised in stalking, train your eyes to be constantly looking ahead, surveying the ground for added cover such as bushes or rocks.

Sound

Wind will also carry sound as well as scent to your quarry, so again make sure you are stalking up-wind. Move carefully and deliberately, so that you make the least possible noise. Watch a cat stalking a mouse and notice how carefully it controls its movements as it slowly glides forward, placing its hind feet in exactly the same place as it put its fore feet.

Sounds at night are much clearer than they are during the day. The rustle of leaves by a hedgehog or shrew makes a startling noise. This is due to your only using one sense,

FOX			Well-marked spoor. Animals killed by a fox are usually without a head and have been dragged some distance.
BADGER			Sow heel-pad smaller in width than boar. Prey usually turned inside out. Hair found on bark, fences and wire.
STOAT			Similar spoor to weasel. Tracks found in ditches and drains.
RABBIT & HARE	LF LH	RABBIT, ORDINARY PACE HARE, ORDINARY PACE	Well-defined spoor. Hare differs from rabbit in spacing of tracks.
SQUIRREL		BOUNDING	Found near trees. Similar to hedgehog but longer toes.
HEDGEHOG	RF RH		Usually found in ditch bottoms.

namely that of hearing, and in consequence every sound is magnified. Of course, there are fewer noises at night, so the ones you hear sound very loud.

On the trail

There are two main ways in which you can go about the observation of nature. One way is to sit down very quietly and wait for something to happen; the second is to walk about and note everything you see.

I would suggest that at first you walk along the trail practising your woodcraft and training your eyes to read the animal sign language. Make notes in your field note-book of all you see and hear.

Later, when you are more experienced, you will go to a particular spot to make a series of observations on a bird or mammal. This will make it necessary to sit quietly for a long period of time in one place; however, this does not mean that you should ignore the other things which are going on round about you. Should you be watching a blackbird feeding its young and counting the number of trips the bird makes carrying food, you can still keep your eyes open for butterflies or watch the shrew that runs across your foot or name the flowers that are growing nearby.

Animal signs along the trail

Warmly dressed and with your field note-book and pencil in your pocket, you start out along a trail through the countryside near your home. Your object is to try to discover the signs or clues left behind by animals. Remember that these signs are everywhere – the countryside is full of birds, beasts and other creatures; and even though you may not see the animals themselves you will certainly see their spoor, hair or droppings if you use your eyes.

4 RECORDING

The field note-book is a naturalist's memory, for in it he records the many interesting animals and plants when he sees them and before he has time to forget all the details. It is so easy to say to yourself: 'I do not need a field note-book; I can easily remember the things I see.' *Do* you remember the colour and field characters of the birds you saw on the table in the garden yesterday? Memory is a very tricky thing and it may let the best naturalist down.

Clear and accurate records are most important, so you should write your field notes while you are actually making your observations. Even the smallest detail, however insignificant it appears, should be noted down. It may seem very unimportant at the time, but later may help you to recall the scene.

When you are out in the country you will see many animals and plants that are new to you, and which you would like to name, so that when you come across them again you will recognize them as old friends. Rather than collect, make detailed descriptions with drawings in your field note-book; and when you arrive home try to identify them from your written notes rather than from specimens. If you can do this you will be sure your notes are accurate observations.

Using the field note-book

When you buy your field note-book, make sure it is stiff-backed, preferably $3\frac{1}{2}$ in. by 5 in. in size. Black is the most

Field Note Book

10 May 1961.

Route Lady Ediths Drive
Bus no 114 — every 15 mins
Raincliffe woods, middle path
Forge Valley bus home — Ayton
united, every half hour

Weather fair wind force 2.
visibility 1 mile.

Companions. John Earnshaw
Norman Sutcliffe, David Colenutt,
Jean Levy.

Observations
1. 10-30 hrs Lady Ediths drive
saw fox tracks in mud at side
of path. Prints in line reading
direction of Wireless Station....

RIGHT HIND PRINTS. TRACKS.

suitable colour, as lighter shades tend to run when they get
wet. There may be a cardboard tube attached to your note-
book to hold your pencil; if not, tie one to the spine of your
book with a length of string. It might be a good idea, particularly if you are out on wet as well as on fine days, to make a
plastic wallet to hold your note-book, or perhaps you could
persuade your father to part with an old tobacco pouch.

The information should be arranged in a special order
starting at the top of the page.

Date
This should be written at the top of the page and include
the day, month and year clearly written in ink before you
leave home.

Route

The general direction of your expedition should be included, giving details of the places you pass through, as well as the number and times of any buses you may use. Bus times are always useful reference notes, as of course are train times; particularly as you might wish to visit the same locality again.

Weather

The weather should most certainly be included and recorded in your notes; it may have a direct bearing on bird movement if it is particularly windy, and on insect numbers if it is humid. The weather may be changeable and you may find it necessary to make several entries in your note-book on the one expedition. Also make notes giving the temperature, cloud forms and wind force.

The wind force can easily be determined by memorizing the Beaufort Table in the official *Meteorological Instruments Handbook*, published by H M Stationery Office. Always use the Beaufort number when making an entry in your note-book and this will save you considerable writing.

Abbreviations

With experience you will invent a system of shorthand which will save time when writing your notes in the field. Two abbreviations used by naturalists, which you might like to use, are the sex signs – male ♂, female ♀.

Time

Not only must you number the paragraphs containing the written details of your observations, but also note down the time that the observation was made. Like the weather, the time may have an important bearing on your observation. Use the Continental time-system, and then there is less chance of your getting your AMs and PMs mixed.

Companions

The names of your companions should also be included in

your field note-book, as you may require them to confirm
your observations at some time in the future.

Location

It is important that you give as accurate a location of your
observation as you can. Normally, you would record that
you saw water violet growing 200 yards downstream on the
west bank, by the alder roots – Forge Valley.

Should you wish to give a more precise location to your
observation you should use the National Grid System
marked on the one-inch-to-the-mile Ordnance Survey
maps.

The National Grid System divides the Ordnance map into
squares by means of lines running north to south and east to
west. Using these lines, you can locate any point by what are
known as four-figure and six-figure references. Write the
sheet number of your map in your field note-book; then
locate the place on the map where you made your observations. Read off the number of the line on the west edge of
the square in which your location occurs (say, for example,
it is 87), then working from the west edge of the square to
the opposite side (the eastern edge), estimate or measure the
number of tenths to your observation point. If it is seven
tenths, your number should read 877. Next read off the
number of the line forming the south edge of your square
(93, for example), and from it estimate or measure the number of tenths northwards to your point. In this case let us say
it is five-tenths. Your second number should read 935. The
two numbers together will give you your six-figure reference
877935. Provided the sheet number of your map is given,
the reference will enable anyone to go to the exact spot
where you made your observations.

To help you in the field, mark both edges of the corner of
a postcard in sixteenths of an inch; when you are finding a
reference, place the corner of the postcard directly on the
spot you want to record and, keeping it in line with the grids,
you will be able to read off the tenths of the grid square
without any difficulty.

Numbers

It is almost impossible to count the total number of birds in one flock, so you must take an estimate. The best way to do this is to count twenty birds and find out how much space they take. Divide the amount of space the twenty birds take up into the total space taken up by the flock. This figure multiplied by twenty will give you a reasonable estimate of the number of birds in the flock.

Height

You may have to estimate the height of a nest in a tree, a flower growing on a cliff, or perhaps a sequence of fossil-bearing deposits for your records. How would you go about it? The easiest way to do this would be to cut a stick five feet long, or alternatively use your thumb stick. Rest the stick

Measuring height

against the tree, and then walk away for twenty or more yards. Holding your pencil out in front of you, measure off the length of the stick on your pencil with your thumb, then measure the number of times that this length of pencil will go into the height of the tree. If it goes into the height of the tree 12 times, multiply that figure by 5, the length in feet of your stick. The height of the tree would then be 60 feet.

The same method can be used equally well on cliffs, outcroppings and even on buildings.

The log-book

As your permanent record, your log-book should be written up as soon as possible after you have arrived home, and while everything is fresh in your mind.

After you have had your meal, make yourself comfortable at a table or desk and neatly copy out your field notes into your log, checking or making identifications and entering the common and scientific names against your written descriptions. You can also copy into your log interesting additional information about the things you have seen, as well as pasting in pictures or photographs relevant to your notes.

The field log should be a hard-backed exercise book – quarto size and preferably ruled. All the pages should be numbered except for the five pages at the end. These five pages should be headed respectively Geology, Plants, Insects, Birds and Mammals, and each page ruled into three columns. This section of the log will serve as an index.

Copy the observations from your field note-book into your log-book in the same form, namely, numbered paragraphs. On the opposite page to your notes mount the illustrations, either press cuttings or your own drawings. Allocate two or more pages to each expedition and rule a red line across the page when the entries for that day in the field have been completed.

Now we come to what is perhaps the most complex part – indexing. As each observation is numbered and written in paragraph form, and each page in the log is numbered, there should be no real difficulty. The first paragraph on page 9 might be an observation on a rookery in Raincliffe Woods; so turn to the five headed pages at the end of the book and make the following entry under BIRDS in the first column:

Rookery, Raincliffe Woods – Page 9/Para 1.

Your second paragraph may be an observation on a Sexton Beetle you found on the banks of Throxenby Mere. Turn to the page headed INSECTS in the index and in the first column make the following entry:

Sexton beetle (burrowing beetle) – Page 9/Para 2.

Gradually you will build an index of observations which will be an invaluable store of knowledge, as well as local records.

Specialist recording

As an older boy or girl specializing in one branch of natural history you might like to keep a third book in which you record observations made only in your own subject. The book should be loose-leaf, with one page devoted to each species. The advantage of a loose-leaf book over a bound book is that you can add more pages as you require them, although its one fault is that the pages will easily come loose.

The disadvantage of a card index is that the cards are usually too small to take a great number of observations.

5 IDENTIFICATION

Scientific names may seem very confusing to you when using reference books for the first time. Yet, with a little study and practice, you will find the scientific names (nomenclature) preferable to the common names. Where there is only one scientific name for an animal, there are two or three common or localized names. For example, the warty newt has one scientific name *Triturus cristatus* Laurenti, but it has several common names – great crested newt and great water newt, to mention only two, and without including the dialect names.

The system of naming that is used by naturalists all over the world is the Binomial (two-named) System. This was devised by the famous Swedish botanist Linnaeus, and first applied by him to the whole of the animal kingdom in the tenth edition of his *System Naturae* published in 1758. By means of this system each animal or plant has two latinized names – a generic and specific name. In the case of the mole, *Talpa europae* L., *Talpa* is the generic name and *europae* the specific name.

The first or generic name is always printed with an initial capital; the second or specific name is printed with a small letter. Usually, the scientific name is printed in italics while the author of the name is printed in Roman type, the author being the first person to designate the name in question and to use it in a printed journal.

In working out a system of classification, scientists have grouped like animals together, forming them into units.

The smallest unit contains the sub-species, but since these are only likely to concern the expert and include a further (trinomial) method of naming, there is no need to mention them here. The next smallest unit is that of the species, a group of similar animals that are capable of breeding among themselves. The species is followed by the genus. The pygmy shrew belongs to the species *minutus* and the genus *Sorex*. Its full scientific name is *Sorex minutus* L., the L. standing for the author, in this case Linnaeus.

The genus *Sorex*, which also includes the common shrew (*Sorex araneus castaneus enyns*) is grouped into the family Soricidae or Shrews. This family links with other families which include moles, bats and hedgehogs, to form the Order Insectivora – a primitive insect-eating group of animals. This order is included with eighteen others to form the class Mammalia, or animals which give milk to their young. Seven classes of animals then make up the subphylum Vertebrata which forms the largest unit of the phylum Chordata or animals with a spinal cord.

Phylum Chordata (animals with nervous cord in the back).
Subphylum Vertebrata (animals with backbone).
Class Mammalia (animals that give milk).
Order Insectivora (primitive insect-eating mammals).
Family Soricidae (Shrews).
Genus Sorex.
Species minutus.

Identifying specimens from books

Many of the standard reference works have keys to help trace down the specimen and its correct scientific name. You will find some keys are easy to use, while others are extremely difficult. It is important initially that you should attempt to memorize the technical names used to describe the parts of an animal or plant, as these are frequently referred to in the key.

The real need in identification is patience, and the young naturalist must be prepared to spend some time in naming his specimens. Mistakes can easily occur, particularly if you are trying to work too quickly, or if you have too much material to identify. Never hurry, and never attempt to do too much.

Often illustrations are used for identification, and this is a mistake. However accurate the colours, they will never give a true representation of the bird, mammal or animal to be identified. Use colour plates by all means for comparison, but rely for specific identification on the descriptions which list the characteristics of the species.

Locality is also important. Many works of reference will give the range of plants or animals, that is to say, whether or not they can be found in your locality. It is no use attempting to identify a flower which you think to be of a certain species, when the book tells you that that species does not exist in your area.

It is essential that your specimens should be identified while they are fresh. Old material is dried and wrinkled, and this makes the task very much more difficult. Normally, naturalists attempt to identify their material on the evening of the day of collection. If this is not possible, then your specimens should be carefully placed in a suitable storage place that will keep them fresh until you are ready to work on them.

Confirm your identification by passing the specimen to an expert. Remember, however, that experts are normally very busy people, so do not take up too much of their time. If you post your specimen, enclose a stamped, addressed envelope or label, and print the full data in your enclosed letter. When your material is returned, do not forget to send a letter of thanks.

PART TWO

6 COLLECTING ROCKS AND FOSSILS

If you make a train journey across your own county, or any part of Britain, you will, provided you are observant, be amazed at the variety of scenery – the hills and mountains, farmlands cut by walls and hedges, the roads, railways and canals, the rolling downs dipping into the wooded valleys where the rivers meander through to the plain, great towns sending smoke into the sky, and among the wastes of the mountain, heather and lichens growing and deer grazing into the wind.

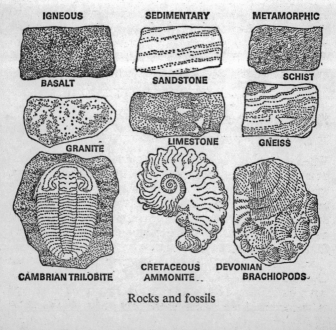

Rocks and fossils

This is your landscape, yet I wonder if you have stopped to ask yourself questions such as: what made the hills and valleys? Why did the towns grow up where we find them today? Why are the hills and mountains sparsely covered with flowers, although the valleys and woodlands abound with vegetation? You will find the answer to these questions on landscape or topography in the study of geology, a natural science which tells the history of the land going back millions of years, far beyond the birth of man.

The geologist fills a vital rôle in our everyday life. Basic industries rely on the skill of the geologist to explore the crust of the earth and find the raw materials which are needed, such as oil, coal, uranium and other ores. Engineers rely on accurate geological information to construct reservoirs and tunnels, and to help in the search for underground water.

During the Second World War, the importance of geology was recognized when specially trained squads were sent to France to collect samples of rock from the Normandy beaches. From this information, special geological maps were drawn of the coastline to assist tank commanders during the landing on D-Day.

Studying the scenery

When walking in the country you should train your eyes to observe the type of rocks that form the landscape. Whenever you notice a change in the scenery, try to find out the cause. Perhaps a band of limestone was responsible for an escarpment being where it is, or marginal land may never have been cultivated because of the infertile soil derived from the gritty underlying rock.

Referring to one of the geological maps produced by the Geological Survey of Great Britain, you will see how outcrops of the same kind of rock will lead to a similar type of scenery in those places where they occur. Notice those rocks which are water holders, and those that are pervious to water. Clay holds water and causes stretches of bogland, while water drains away through sandstone, making this healthier land on which to live. Water in granite country is always pure, while that from chalk or limestone is 'hard' owing to the quantities of calcareous matter dissolved in it.

As your interest in geology grows you will find that this science has been split into a number of special studies:

Petrology: the study of rocks, their properties and composition.

Palaeontology: the study of animal life found as fossils in the rocks.

Stratigraphy: the study of rocks as they occur in layers of strata in the earth's crust.

Applied geology: aspects of geology that are useful in mining, engineering and agriculture.

Of these, the two that you will probably find of most interest are petrology and palaeontology. The collection of fossils or rock specimens makes a fascinating hobby and one that can be followed in any area and at very little expense.

Petrology

To a geologist, the term 'rock' can signify anything from a piece of granite or limestone, to a deposit of sand, mud or gravel. There are three general types of rock: igneous, metamorphic, and sedimentary.

Igneous rocks
If you obtain a piece of granite and examine it carefully, there are a number of things that will strike you immediately. You will see that it is a hard rock composed of three different kinds of crystalline particles. Each kind is distin-

guished by its colour, size and shape. The three minerals making up the granite are:

Quartz – colourless and transparent.
Felspar – white, grey or pink.
Mica – grey-brown, black.

Granite is an example of one of the igneous rocks, that solidified from a molten mass. On cooling, crystals formed, and with practice these can be recognized and the specimens identified. There are a number of ways by which you can identify minerals, by their colour, hardness, crystalline form and specific gravity.

Lavas from volcanoes are igneous rocks too. The molten lava cooled quickly on exposure to the atmosphere, and thus the crystals did not have time to grow large, and the lava is said to be fine-grained, ie, made up of small crystals. By contrast the molten mass which gave rise to granites cooled slowly in the depths of the earth, so that the crystals had time to grow big, and granite is a coarse-grained rock.

Metamorphic rocks
These are rocks that have been altered by heat and pressure. Heat causes the crystals to break down and re-crystallize, often into simpler and more stable forms. Pressure causes the crystals to arrange themselves with their longest axis at right angles to the seat of pressure.

Sedimentary rocks
These rocks are formed under water from the sediment brought down from the existing rocks. Limestones, shales and sandstones were formed either in seas, estuaries or lakes millions of years ago.

Palaeontology

By your study of fossils you will come to understand the animal and plant life of past ages, when conditions were vastly different from those of today.

Fossils, you will find, are remains of plants and animals preserved in sedimentary rocks. These can take a number of forms.

The most commonly found fossil is the cast, where the animal or vegetable body decayed, and the internal structure of the organism was completely replaced by rock, or by minerals in solution such as iron compounds and silica. In other cases, the internal structure of the animal or plant was replaced by minerals in solution, but was not changed. By this last method of fossilization, or petrefaction, the complete structure of the animal or plant is retained, and the palaeontologist can section a fossil and examine the structure with a microscope, very much as he would living specimens. More recent fossils are preserved exactly as in life, such as mammals preserved completely in ice as on the day they died. Peat is vegetation which, subject to pressure, has become semi-fossilized, yet retains its structure. Insects from the Baltic have been trapped and preserved by resin on pine trees. Today, this hardened resin is called amber.

If you search the right deposits you may even find the casts made by worms on sand many millions of years ago (very much like those made by the lug worm on our seashores today), or the footprints left behind by the giant dinosaur as it walked across a muddy estuary. These are fossils, just as much as the ammonite or the sea shells that you find, and, as such, should be preserved.

Collecting
To collect fossils or rocks you must have a knowledge of the locality you are going to search, as well as the type of rocks that you are likely to find. Such rocks as granite or

marble, formed under very great heat and pressure, contain no fossils; but fossils can be found in most limestones, clays and shales which were all formed by sediments deposited on the bed of seas, lakes or estuaries. The equipment you will need is:

Field note-book and pencil.

Geological map. The most suitable geological map for your purpose will be the one produced by the Geological Survey of the 'Solid' rocks of your area. A Survey 'Drift' map records the overlying boulder clays, sands, gravels and other deposits laid down during the Ice Ages.

Geological hammer. A good type of hammer for all geological purposes has a head which is square in section, cut at one end to a square face, and at the other to a chisel edge made at right angles to the shaft. The hammer should be two to three pounds in weight. It is used for breaking off lumps from an exposure using the square edge, while the other end is useful for splitting shales or sandstones. Some

Geological equipment

geologists carry a second, smaller hammer for splitting or trimming the rough material they have obtained with their larger, heavier hammer.

Compass. This is useful when drawing rough plans in your field note-book, and also for getting the direction or lie of the quarry.

Roll of Elastoplast (used in labelling specimens) and a razor blade.

A number of linen or canvas collecting bags. These are useful for carrying the material home and can be purchased from geological dealers. Alternatively you can make effective use of blue sugar bags.

Cold chisels of varying sizes.

In the field

Using your one-inch-to-the-mile Ordnance Survey map, list the quarries in your area; compare the site of each quarry with a Geological 'Solid' map, and you will find out the nature of the rocks in each of the listed quarries. From this inquiry and with suitable text-books you will know the type of fossils you are likely to find there. The Geological Survey Handbook for your area, costing about 30p (HMSO), will be particularly valuable.

When you set out to collect in the field, besides the equipment you are carrying in your haversack, you will need comfortable old boots or shoes, and old clothes. Examination of rock faces can be dirty and dusty work, and you should prepare yourself before you start. A word of warning too – quarries can be very dangerous places, particularly after storms and frost when rock is likely to have been loosened.

Always make a practice of seeking permission to enter quarries that you wish to examine, and ask the foreman whether it is safe or not to work the quarry face. In this way you will gain the respect of the quarry owner, his foreman and workmen, and they may be helpful in finding and retaining specimens for you to examine. Do not go if you are told not to.

When you arrive at the quarry, make a small map of the

area in your field note-book. Plot the nearest trees, church or houses, marking the position of the quarry on the map in relation to the surrounding topography, as well as the local names that are important. Always remember to put a compass direction or bearing on your map in the top right-hand corner, as well as an indication of the scale.

After you have planned the area to a reasonably large scale, make a preliminary survey of the quarry face. Without hurrying, and as though you have all the time in the world, note the number and position of the different layers of rock, whether or not they are sedimentary rocks, and the number of different kinds of fossils they contain. A survey of this sort is very important, as the knowledge that you gain from it builds up a picture in your own mind of the history or nature of the deposit, completing a picture of the conditions that existed many millions of years ago when those deposits were laid down.

With your preliminary survey over, make a careful sketch in your field note-book of the quarry face, the kinds of rocks exposed, the way in which they are laid down and the direction that the strata or beds of rock take. The sketches should be sufficiently large to allow you the opportunity later of entering notes on the specimens that you collect, and the measurements of the different layers. Add remarks about the colour of the rocks, as well as details of gravel, clays, etc, that you can see at the top or the section.

After you have made your preliminary recordings you can collect your material, using your large hammer and chisels. The advantage of using a chisel is that you can place it directly on the spot you wish to hit, without endangering a fossil. It is always wise to collect a piece larger than the fossil itself: this can be trimmed down later without the risk of damaging the specimen.

As each specimen is obtained it should be numbered. This is done by cutting a small piece of Elastoplast, sticking it on the specimen, and, using a biro pen, marking it with a number. Enter the same number in your field note-book, and add a note as to the strata it came from and its associated material. Next, you must mark the position and number of the fossil on your sketch map of the quarry face. Write as many details as you possibly can about your find.

Place the fossil in one of the linen bags and put it in your rucksack. When you are collecting fossils do not forget to examine the quarry floor, turning over the fallen, weathered rocks. This may save you a great deal of work.

Recording

At home, you can record permanently the details of a quarry on an index card, or in a loose-leaf note-book. At the top of your card or page, enter the name of the quarry, and below, copy out your sketch map of the area, and the section of the quarry face; use Indian ink and the symbols that have been adopted for the principal types of rocks.

The shading of rocks on diagrams of this nature is based on simple characters that are uniform throughout geological illustrations. Shales are always illustrated by close-set lines parallel to the lay of the bed. Sandstones are shown by layers of dots, their thickness illustrating the nature of the sandstone as to whether it is coarse or fine. Limestones are illustrated by means of a brick pattern that again follows the slope of the strata. Igneous or volcanic rocks are shown by means of short dashes arranged in all directions. You should use these symbols whenever you can, and after a while they will become second nature to you.

Make your final recording as detailed as you possibly can, copying out all the information from your field note-book carefully, as well as listing the fossils you have obtained from the quarry.

The data should be entered on each specimen you have collected. This can be done quite simply by dabbing a spot of paint on the side of the fossil where it will not matter, and writing on it the full data with a mapping pen, using Indian ink. When both the paint and the Indian ink are dry, cover with gold size. The data should include the following:

Scientific name.
Locality.

Collector's name.
Date.

Storage

As the fossils in your collection will be of different sizes, you
will have to store them in a cabinet or a chest of drawers.
The ordinary household drawers are very suitable for this
purpose, and with cardboard or plywood they can be divided
into small sections, each section to hold one or more fossils.

Arrange your collection in the drawers according to their
family or the strata from which they were obtained.

Label each specimen carefully, and card-index the collection for easy reference.

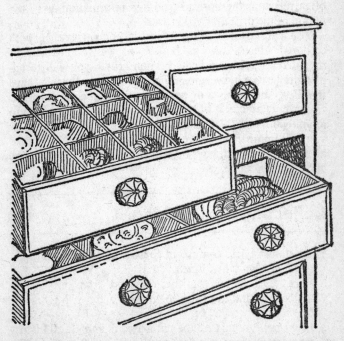

Geological specimens stored in chest of drawers adapted for
the purpose

7 COLLECTING AND MOUNTING PLANTS

You will find the identification of flowering plants in the field will not only be great fun but an important part of your natural history. If you collect butterflies or moths you must know the flowering plants, otherwise you will not be able to find the eggs, larvae and pupae of the insects. The geologist often relies on the flora to give him information as to the nature of the drift and solid rocks.

You will start identifying flowers by comparing them with coloured illustrations in books. As your collection of mounted wild flowers or herbarium grows, you will recognize similarities between one specimen and another. Perhaps it will be the number of petals, or the shape of the stem; whatever character it is, it will indicate a feature common to a family of plants. When you see a plant with that character you will immediately recognize its family and, with a suitable reference work, have no difficulty in finding its scientific and common name.

Collecting equipment

The botanist's field equipment consists of the following:

Field note-book and pencil.

Price tags. These can be obtained from a shop in your locality, and are used to attach to the plant for the data.

Vasculum. Vascula can be purchased from natural history dealers, or alternatively they can be devised from long, flat biscuit tins or polythene bags.

Sharp knife or trowel. These are used for digging up plants.
Hand lens.
National Grid map. This is useful to give a grid reference
when recording a locality.

Collecting

When you collect in the field it is important to remember to
take the complete plant, including the flower, stem, leaves,
fruit and roots. Many of the characters used in the identification of plants will necessitate your possessing the
complete specimen.

Important: if you find a rare plant you should resist the
temptation to collect it, and content yourself by taking
detailed field notes. All too frequently, the unthinking
eagerness of the collector has prevented some rare plant
from re-establishing itself in old haunts, or from extending
its range to new ones.

Select the most suitable specimen.

Using the trowel or knife, carefully dig round the roots
and lift the plant out.

Shake the loose soil from the roots.

Taking a label from your haversack, attach it to the stem
of the plant so that it will not shake loose. In pencil, enter
the following details on the label: specimen number (if it is
the first specimen you have taken that day, it will be specimen no 1); detailed locality; name of the specimen if it is
known; and the date.

After you have completed the price tag attached to the
specimen, you should enter the details in your field note-
book. Notes on the habitat must be as full as you can make
them, if possible locating the exact situation, using a six-
figure map reference (see page 23) to site the plant. The
weather exercises a decided influence on plants, therefore
your notes should contain accurate weather readings. Other
notes should include altitude, soil details, the colour of the

plant, whether it is early or late flowering, and additional information on the surrounding flora.

Wrap your specimen in damp blotting paper, newspaper, moss or grass and gently place it in your vasculum or collecting tin.

Pressing equipment

The equipment you will need to press and mount the flowering plants you have collected is a little more comprehensive than that used in collecting in the field. Much of it can be made at home with a little initiative. The items include:

Plant press. This, as the name implies, is a piece of apparatus in which flowers are dried and flattened. A press need only consist of two boards measuring 12in. by 15in. Attach tape to the boards. Leave 3 to 6in. of tape overhanging at each side of the board for tying. Alternatively, you might like to use strong elastic bands, and these can be adapted from the inner tubes of car tyres cut into one-inch strips. A third method is to use butterfly screws at each corner. The bolts should be firmly fitted to the lower board, the top board having four corresponding holes to slip the bolts through.

Drying paper. The purpose of drying paper is to absorb the moisture, under pressure, from the plant. Drying paper is sold by natural-history dealers, but white blotting paper is equally effective and less costly.

Newspaper. Newspaper is used as additional packing to separate the drying specimens that have been placed between the blotting or drying paper. Cut sheets of newspaper to the size of the press, 12in. by 15in., and have a considerable quantity on hand ready for the time when you commence to press your collected specimens.

Mounting paper. Cartridge paper, cut to a standard size, makes ideal mounting paper. The most suitable size for your herbarium sheets would be 8in. by 12in. From one sheet of cartridge paper you will get four pieces of mounting paper.

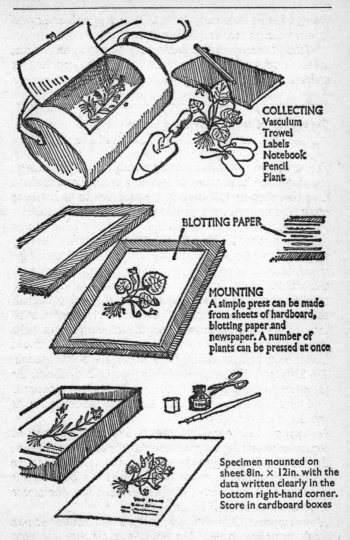

COLLECTING
Vasculum
Trowel
Labels
Notebook
Pencil
Plant

BLOTTING PAPER

MOUNTING
A simple press can be made from sheets of hardboard, blotting paper and newspaper. A number of plants can be pressed at once.

Specimen mounted on sheet 8in. × 12in. with the data written clearly in the bottom right-hand corner. Store in cardboard boxes

Labels. Data labels to stick on the sheet of paper with the mounted specimen are not necessarily essential. Data can be written clearly in the bottom right-hand corner of the mounting paper.

Folders. These can be used to store your mounted specimens. They should be of a standard size and the specimens should be filed away in the folders under Families. Write clearly on the outside of each folder the name of the Family.

Naphthalene. Naphthalene is used, scattered in the folders, to prevent mites attacking the specimens. White or transparent adhesive paper is used to attach dried specimens to the mounting paper. Economy envelope labels make an effective adhesive. Cut the economy labels into thin strips a quarter of an inch wide. Store them in a box ready for use.

Identification

Specimens should be identified before they are mounted, and while they are still fresh. Try to identify your specimens as soon as you arrive home, using the standard works listed in Appendix B.

Pressing method

Lay the bottom board of the plant press on the table. Spread three or four of the cut pieces of newspaper on the board, and then a sheet of blotting paper.

Take the flowers to be preserved and dry carefully, using blotting paper or a clean cloth; work over the leaves and stem very gently. It may be necessary to wash specimens prior to mounting or pressing them. In this case, hold the specimen under the tap for a few seconds, then thoroughly dry off and leave in the sun for a short time before pressing.

Take the flower you are preserving and put it on the blotting paper with the head of the plant to the left. Arrange the plant in a natural position. Place an upright plant straight on the page with a margin at top and bottom. Let the head of a snowdrop or harebell droop, or a spray of wild clematis trail down across the page. A tall plant will need to be pressed in two parts, one with flower and bud, upper stalk and leaves, and then beside it the lower leaves and root. Before pressing a bushy plant, some of the leaves should be picked off.

When the plant has been placed in a roughly natural position, arrange the stems, petals and leaves with a fine paint brush, then immediately cover them with scraps of clean blotting paper. A small piece should be put between the top and bottom petals of a flower that is pressed closed.

When the plant has been arranged, cover with a second piece of blotting paper, or drying paper. Put another four sheets of newspaper, or more for a thick plant, carefully over it, and a sheet of blotting paper on that, and continue with the next specimen.

Note: you should make sure that all parts of the plant get equal pressure. Let us suppose you are pressing an ox-eye daisy. Arrange it on the drying sheet; cut a circular piece of blotting paper with a hole in the centre, and put it over the flower. A similar-shaped piece of cotton wool is placed over that, and the white florets will then receive the same pressure as the golden centre. Large buds should be treated in the same way, and this applies also to the fruit or seed pods.

When all the flowers have been arranged, place the second board of the press in position, fasten the two boards together and tighten them. Then add weights to the board. Large flat stones, or books, are ideally suited as weights.

The drying papers must be changed frequently, otherwise the flowers lose their colour and turn brown. Yellow-flowered and dry wiry plants can be left unchanged for 24 hours, while others will need changing in 4 to 12 hours. The moister the plant, the more often it will need new drying papers.

As soon as the plant is thoroughly dry, it should be taken

from the press and stored away between newspapers ready
for mounting. Some plants will be ready after about the
fourth change of drying papers. If you find the flowers are
not absolutely dry, leave them for a little longer, otherwise
they will suffer from mildew.

If there is to be some time lag between removing the
flowers from the press and mounting them, place them in a
second press between sheets of white paper. Place them in an
air-tight cupboard and scatter naphthalene over and around
the press. This will exclude mites or minute insects from
attacking them. On the whole, however, it is always best to
mount your specimens as soon as possible. This not only
guards against their becoming damaged, but will also get
you into the habit of working methodically and carefully.

Mounting

Place the pressed flower on the piece of mounting paper, and
arrange it in as natural a position as possible. Mount only
one specimen to a sheet of mounting paper.

Mark lightly in pencil the position of the stalk, leaves and
flowers.

Place the plant face-downwards on newspaper and carefully cover it with herbarium paste, gloy or gum tragacanth
solution.

Lay the plant on the mounting paper, positioning it to the
pencil marks. Cover with blotting paper and smooth down.

Cover with newspaper, then with a piece of cardboard,
and add weights. (An alternative and quicker method is to
fasten the specimen down with the strips of gummed paper,
preferably transparent, but non-cellulose. The strips should
be laid carefully across the stems.)

Examine the plant after three hours and re-paste any part
that has not stuck.

Labelling and recording

After mounting your specimens, prepare a botanical label, or enter the data in the bottom right-hand corner of the sheet. The data should consist of the following information taken from the price tag and field note-book:

Common name.	Date.
Scientific name.	Collector.
Family.	Associated herbage.
Locality.	Specimen number.

Final recording can be done either on an index card or in a loose-leaf note-book under Species. The card or page should be ruled into five columns, headed respectively: Specimen number, Date, Detailed locality, Collector, Information.

The information should be copied from the field note-book and should be as informative as possible, showing whether a specimen is new to a locality, if it is exceptionally early or late in flowering, the altitude at which it was obtained, and the nature of the soil or underlying rock. Details of the surrounding flora might also be entered.

Storage

Specimens should be handled carefully, as they become quite brittle after a period of time. A successful way of storing your material is in cardboard folders – one folder to a Family. As your collection grows, more folders can be added at little cost. Label each folder carefully in Indian ink and store in a dry air-tight cupboard.

SPECIAL NOTES

Grasses

These are pressed and mounted in the same way as wild flowers and ferns. It is important to note that, as they dry very quickly, very few changes of drying paper are required. Hold the specimen to the mounting paper by means of strips placed across at various points.

Ferns

There are about forty species of British ferns, a number of which are quite rare. Their method of reproduction, as well as their structure, makes them a fascinating hobby for the botanist.

Ferns are mounted in very much the same way as wild flowers, and are pressed in a botanical press. Owing to the large size of the fronds of many ferns, it is necessary for the boards forming the press to be larger than those used for wild flowers (18in. by 12in. will accommodate most of the fronds of the larger species).

Try to mount two fronds to a sheet, one with the top surface uppermost, and one with the lower or under surface uppermost, showing sori.

Fungi

Toadstools or fungi are very difficult to preserve. There is, however, a method by which you can record the fungi that you find growing in the woods and hedgerows during autumn. Specimens can be collected and brought home for identification, and details can be entered up on a large index card, or a sheet of white cardboard.

Collecting

Using a knife, carefully lift out the best specimen of each species you find.

Make out on a price label all the data necessary to the find, the exact location of the specimen, collector's name and the date. At the same time, enter full details in your field notebook.

Wrap the specimen with the attached price label in newspaper, and place it in either a basket or your haversack. Small specimens can be placed in tins.

Recording

When you get your specimens home, clean them carefully by washing, and then section one of each of the species you have collected.

Draw on the record card, a section of the fungus, accurately noting the way the gills are attached to the stem.

Taking another fungus of the same species, cut off the umbrella-like top, and place it, gills down, on a piece of white drawing paper, putting a jam jar over the cap to keep it moist. Later (24 hours), lift the cap and you will find a coloured pattern formed by the tiny particles or spores from the gills of the fungus. From the second specimen, scrape the spores into a small heap, and place for further reference in a small envelope.

While waiting for the spore print you can draw the fungus, and colour with either water colour or crayons. Try to do this from as many different positions as you can.

Carefully pour water, to which glue has been added, over the spore print and leave on one side to dry.

Using the reference books listed in Appendix B, try to find out the name of the specimen, not only its common name but its scientific name too.

When the print is dry, collect all your notes and drawings

together and add them to the sheet of white cardboard or record card. Put at the top the common name of the fungus, and the scientific name underneath, followed by a detailed description of the locality in which you found the fungus, whenever possible noting associated plants, particularly trees. Glue your drawing on to the card and attach the spore print. Add information about the smell of the fungus, as well as detailed measurements as to the width of the cap, the height of the fungus and accurate notes on its colouring.

Seaweeds

Many seaweeds make satisfactory herbarium specimens. The following details give you the methods used in collecting and preserving these algae from the sea.

Gather your seaweed and bring home damp in a vasculum or collecting tin.

Wash quickly in salt water. Larger specimens should be soaked for three to four hours to prevent them retaining a coating of salt.

Float the specimens in a second dish of salt water. Fresh water causes the specimens to disintegrate.

Taking a sheet of mounting paper, place it underneath the floating plant. Then slip a glass plate, or a sheet of perforated zinc beneath the paper.

While the plant is in this position and partly submerged in the water, yet attachable to the paper, you can arrange the specimen, using a mounted surgical needle or a fine brush with bristles spread out.

Remove the mounting paper and the specimen from the water and lay on a thin piece of blotting paper.

Lay a thin piece of muslin over the specimen and cover with another piece of blotting paper and a wad of newspaper. Repeat this process for the number of specimens you have collected. Finally, replace the top of your press and add a suitable weight.

Change the drying papers regularly, every day in the week, until the plants are dry.

The larger, more bulky seaweeds can be attached to the mounting paper using gloy, Higgins vegetable glue or any clean adhesive.

Write the data at the bottom right-hand corner of the sheet in the same way as you would for wild flowers.

Mosses and lichens

Mosses
Mosses should be collected, air dried, wrapped in paper and then transferred to envelopes. Data should be written clearly on the top left-hand corner of the envelope before the specimens are filed away in a cabinet drawer for reference.

Lichens
Most lichens are attached to rocks. Preservation is unnecessary with lichens, provided the specimens are kept in a dry condition. You should try to take as thin a sliver of rock as possible, storing as for mosses in an envelope with the data in the top left-hand corner, and filing in a cabinet drawer.

8 COLLECTING AND MOUNTING INSECTS

Introduction

Insects are everywhere, and form four-fifths of the animal population of the world. Yet, although they occur in such large numbers, and are so widely spread over the face of the earth, there is a great deal still to learn about the life history and even the habits of most insects. The young naturalist interested in entomology, as the study of insect life is called,

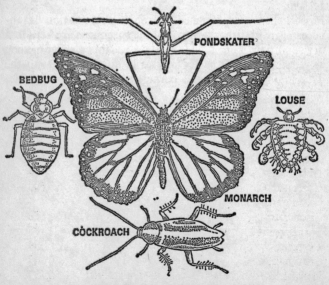

A butterfly and some beetles

can perform a valuable service to natural history by observing, collecting and carefully recording, thereby helping, as an entomologist, to fill the gaps in our knowledge.

No boy or girl will be able to collect and study all the insects in the British Isles. There are 20,000 species so far known, and even to adult entomologists most of these are known only as names in catalogues or as mounted specimens in large collections. To make a successful collection, the young naturalist will have to specialize in one Order of insects, such as butterflies and moths (Lepidoptera), beetles (Coleoptera) or flies (Diptera).

The following list will serve as a guide to the Orders of the largest British insects and those which can be readily collected and preserved by the methods described in this chapter.

Although specializing in your collections, you should familiarize yourself with the insects of all the following orders:

Orders of Insects	Common Name	No of British Species
Orthoptera	Cockroaches, grass-hoppers	38
Dermaptera	Earwigs	9
Plecoptera	Stoneflies	32
Ephemeroptera	Mayflies	46
Odonata	Dragonflies	42
Hemiptera/Heteroptera	Bugs	499
Hemiptera/Homoptera	Greenfly; scale insects	912
Megaloptera	Alderflies; snakeflies	6
Neuroptera	Lacewings; ant-lions	54
Coleoptera	Beetles	3,690
Mecoptera	Scorpionflies	4
Trichoptera	Caddisflies	188
Lepidoptera	Butterflies and moths	2,187
Diptera	True flies	5,199
Siphonaptera	Fleas	47
Hymenoptera	Bees, wasps, ants and ichneumon flies	6,191

The general principles of collecting and mounting detailed in the following pages for Lepidoptera and Coleoptera apply equally to the other Orders listed above.

BUTTERFLIES AND MOTHS

The most beautiful and spectacular of the insects are the butterflies and moths, which form the Order Lepidoptera (scale wings). The young naturalist who collects insects in this Order is known as a lepidopterist. The chief differences between butterflies and moths can be summarized as follows:

Butterflies	Moths
Sub-Order – Rhopalocera	Sub-Order – Heterocera
Antennae clubbed and held erect.	Antennae generally taper to a point, except burnets, which thicken towards the tip, but are not actually clubbed.
Butterflies have pinched-in waist.	Moths have no waist.
Wings raised erect over body when at rest.	Usually wings laid flat – fore wings covering hind wings.

The life cycle of butterflies and moths is called a *complete metamorphosis*. The egg or ovum (plural ova) is laid on or near the food plant. The caterpillar or larva (plural larvae) hatches from the egg and in most cases eats its own eggshell and then feeds on the food plant, changing or moulting its skin as it grows. After the final moult it becomes a chrysalis or pupa (plural pupae). The pupa is a stage of inactivity when the larva changes into the adult butterfly or moth, known as the imago (plural imagines). The complete metamorphosis may take only a few days, or as long as a year.

To make a complete collection you must not only collect

the adult insect or imago, but also the ova, larva and pupa. To do this successfully you must know at what time of the year to go collecting the food plants of the various species in order to obtain ova and larvae, and where to look for the imagines.

All too often an enthusiastic young naturalist, who sets out to make a collection of butterflies and moths, quickly tires when he finds the same species of butterfly in his net time after time. To collect methodically you must know where in your area to search.

Local knowledge

There are three sources of information available to the young naturalist: these are the local museum, the natural history societies and local records.

Museums
Many museums possess reference or student collections of animals, including insects, that occur locally. Explain your interest in Lepidoptera to the curator or keeper of the museum and he will not only encourage you, but, if you are a sufficiently serious lepidopterist, will allow you to see the collections. When you examine the collections, notice when (DATE) and where (LOCALITY) each specimen was obtained. Make a note of these points in your note-book and try to visit the localities on or about the same date, and if the weather is suitable, you may see the insects on the wing.

Natural history societies
When you next visit your public library, ask the librarian if there are any natural history societies in your area, and when and where they meet. There are many societies of this kind in the British Isles, all of whom would willingly welcome you as a junior member, and encourage your interest in this branch of natural history.

Local records
County societies, local societies and students, keep either written or published records of the local insect fauna of a district. Records of this nature are invaluable, as the date and locality are given with each species listed.

Prospecting

With the knowledge you have obtained from your local museum or natural history society, you should be ready for work in the field. It is a good plan to prospect the area where you intend to collect. Try to get some idea what sort of collecting ground it will be. Study the flowering plants of the neighbourhood: notice whether it is open or close woodland, boggy or dry, sheltered or windy. Identify insects that are flying, and notice their particular haunts. Many butterflies often return to the same place – a patch of flowers or a twig. Fritillaries and White Admirals pass through open spaces in woods time after time.

The following situations are suitable for good collecting: open woodlands, heaths and moors during windy weather; hedges, not too high or dense; fens and bogs with plenty of reeds and bulrushes; ponds and borders of streams where there is plenty of vegetation at the edges, and aquatic plants on or under the water; sand-hills and cliffs at the seaside; chalk pits and gravel pits; mountain sides with varied flora; waste ground overgrown with ragwort and thistles, and banks covered with common flowering plants.

A prospecting visit to an area will give you a knowledge of the character and flora of the countryside in which you are going to collect. With this knowledge, and suitable reference works, you can find which species of butterfly and moth you are most likely to observe, and the best time to collect specimens.

The junior naturalist must remember that it does not always follow that the insects are sure to be found at that particular time. The weather controls butterflies and moths

to a great extent. A prevailing wind may delay the appear-
ance of a species for a number of weeks, while warm, wet
weather is very productive.

Searching

Butterflies love sunshine, and they can be spotted easily
with a little experience. Moths, on the other hand, are difficult to see, and the young naturalist will have to search
carefully for them. The following are likely places:

Trunks of trees
These should be carefully searched: anything having a
triangular shape or outline should be carefully examined.
Certain moths carry their wings erect when drying them, so
the tree should be examined from several feet away. Examine the trunk carefully about 3 feet from the ground, as
this is where many species rest. On a windy night, search the
sheltered side of the trunk.

Palings
Examine all palings very carefully. The top ledge is a likely
spot in spring and autumn. Outhouses, barns, the underside
of window sills and copings are satisfactory collecting places
after a high wind. The young naturalist should always make
a point of examining the sunny, windward side of fences as
often as possible.

Collecting equipment

Note-book and pencil.	Paper – 3in. by 5in.
Sweep net.	Walking stick.
Butterfly net.	Tobacco tin.
Glass-bottomed pill boxes.	Forceps.
Killing bottle.	Needle and thread.

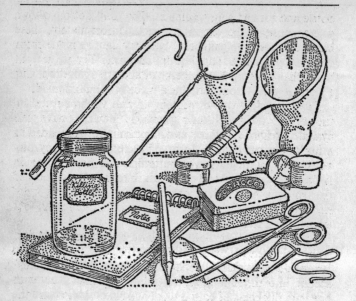

Collecting equipment for insects

Many of the articles of equipment necessary for collecting can be made by a boy or girl at very little cost.

Field note-book. See page 20.

Sweep net. This can be made by sewing a pear-shaped bag of strong calico, measuring about 15in. by 30in., and fixing it to an old tennis racket frame. It should be sewn securely, or it will tear loose.

Butterfly net. This should not only have a large mouth, but should be quite deep. A useful size would be 15in. across the mouth and 30in. deep. The net should again be pear-shaped and made from a light but serviceable material. Nylon window netting with a mesh of 15 to 25 threads per inch is excellent for the purpose. The frame can be made from cane, the ends of which fit into a hollow brass Y or wire.

Glass-bottomed pill box. Glass-bottomed pill boxes are essential, both for transferring specimens from net to killing bottle and for carrying specimens. The glass bottom allows you to observe the captured insect. Unfortunately, these boxes are costly to purchase, but they can be made from ordinary pill boxes, supplied by chemists. Try to get pill boxes that measure 2in. in diameter and are 1½in. deep. Cut a circle in the bottom and glue a piece of celluloid inside.

Killing bottle. I would recommend that young naturalists use ethyl acetate to kill their specimens. You may have seen cyanide, crushed laurel leaves or ammonia recommended in other books on natural history, but they have many disadvantages, particularly with butterflies and moths. Cyanide is deadly poisonous and ammonia bleaches the colour of the specimens. Crushed cherry laurel deteriorates very rapidly, is not sufficiently powerful to kill large moths, but is useful as a relaxing agent.

To make a killing bottle, procure a wide-mouthed jar, with a close-fitting screw cap or cork. A honey or pickle jar would be suitable. Pour half a teaspoonful of ethyl acetate into the killing bottle, and cover immediately with one inch thickness of cotton wool and linen. Make sure the padding is well rammed down with a flat surface. If condensation occurs in the killing bottle, place blotting paper round the inside wall of the jar. It is often a good policy, when there is more than one specimen in the jar at a time, loosely to screw some tissue paper and place it in the jar. This gives the specimens something to climb on to, and stops them rubbing against each other.

Folding paper. Folding paper is used to carry dead specimens safely home.

Pieces of paper 24in. by 3in. are suitable to the purpose and are folded as illustrated on page 62. The papered butterflies or moths are then carefully packed in a square tobacco tin.

Walking stick. A walking stick is always a useful item in the young lepidopterist's equipment, and serves to hook down branches and beat herbage. An enterprising young naturalist might even devise the method of attaching the nets to the ferrule end of the walking stick.

Forceps. Although entomological forceps are rather expensive, they have been designed especially for entomological work – lifting pinned specimens and mounting. They are therefore a necessary item in the young entomologist's equipment.

Needle and thread. These are always useful in repairing a torn net.

Collecting

It is quite an art to net and box a butterfly or moth without damaging it. Usually, in the excitement of the chase, the young naturalist tires himself and frightens the insect. Approach the butterfly or moth cautiously, with the net fully extended; as the insect is swept into the net, continue your sweep and the butterfly will fly down to the bottom of the net; then gradually turn the handle so that the mouth of the net is horizontal. The insect will rest securely at the bottom of the bag.

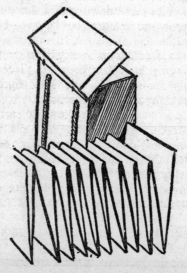

To transfer the insect to the killing bottle, use one of the glass-bottomed pill boxes. Remove the lid and hold it in your left hand. With the pill box in your right hand, carefully work it down the net towards the insect. Cover the butterfly with the pill box, pulling the net tight over the top to act as a temporary lid, while you work your left hand down to slide the lid onto the pill box. If the transfer is accomplished carefully, the insect will not have taken fright and damaged itself.

When it is in the pill box, examine the butterfly through the celluloid base. If you already have the species represented in your collection, do not hesitate to let it go.

It is at this point, while you are examining your specimen, that you should ask yourself, 'Why was that butterfly here?' The answer to that question raises further questions, which you can only answer by careful examination of the specimen and the surrounding vegetation. These questions are:

Is it freshly emerged?
Is it a female laying eggs?
Is it flying about its food plant?
Is it enjoying the sunshine?
Is it its proper time of flight?
Was it frightened?

The answers to these questions may decide you to examine the grass, flowering plants and bushes about the site of your capture. If your specimen is a newly emerged imago, examination might reveal other insects bursting out of their pupal skins. An adult female, on the other hand, might have been ovipositing or laying her eggs on a plant in the area.

If the specimen is one that you need in your collection, transfer it from the pill box to the killing jar. When the insect is dead transfer it carefully to a piece of the folding paper, and fold as illustrated on page 62. Number and write the following data on the flap:

County.
Locality (detailed).
Date.

When you have done this, make a full entry in your field

note-book, including a detailed description of the site of capture. Preface your entry with the *number* of the specimen. The number is important as it links the specimen with the field note-book entry. The first capture of the day is No 1, and so on.

Additional collecting methods

Sugaring
This process, used by lepidopterists, involves the use of brown sugar and black treacle as the basic ingredients, with the addition of a teaspoonful of rum. This semi-liquid is painted on trees and palings to attract night-flying moths.

Sugaring – note the mining helmet with lamp attachment

The sugaring mixture is really too messy to make at home, unless you have a suitable outbuilding. The mixture can be purchased from one or other of the natural-history dealers (see Appendix F).

Before you begin sugaring, collect your equipment. You will need sugaring mixture, an old paintbrush, a torch, pill boxes and, most important of all, overalls to protect your clothes.

The evenings most suitable for sugaring are warm, dark ones with a cloudy sky. Even during heavy rain insects will swarm on sugar. Avoid bright moonlight evenings, cold weather and ground fogs.

Never sugar in woods that are too dense.

Sugar at dusk, choosing trees that have the roughest bark, such as elm, oak, poplar, and silver birch on moorland. The sugar should be put on a patch 6in. by 2in., level with the eyes. If there are no trees, palings and bushes, some of the tall flowering plants can be sugared.

The difficulty is in boxing the moths feeding on the sugar. Holding your torch in your left hand, raise it slowly up the trunk, while you manipulate the pill box and lid with the right hand. This may sound tricky (see illustration on page 65), but the pill box can easily be opened and shut with one hand. Do not shine the light directly on the sugar, but raise it slowly up the trunk.

Speed is essential in examining the patch to see which specimens you consider worth taking and boxing, before the moths get too skittish.

Sugaring by day will attract certain butterflies.

Light
Night-flying moths are dazzled by light, yet are attracted to it, as you will know from the specimens seen flying around the electric light bulb, particularly if the window is left open on a mild summer evening.

The young naturalist can devise a simple light trap, which will attract and hold a number of unusual moths that he would otherwise have difficulty in obtaining.

Setting equipment

Forceps.	Tobacco tin with papered specimens.
Setting board.	Field note-book.
Setting needles.	Mapping pen.
Pins.	Indian ink.
Tracing paper.	Hooked needle for pulling out legs.
Data labels.	

As with the collecting equipment, the material used in setting butterflies and moths can be made by a boy or girl at very little cost.

Forceps. (See page 61.)

Setting board. Setting boards can be made at home by the young naturalist. As the size of Lepidoptera varies from the large-bodied Hawkmoths to the small Blues and even smaller Micro-moths, you will have to make several setting boards, each of a different width and groove (for the body). The one I shall describe here is suitable for Red Admiral or Tortoise-shells. Obtain a piece of soft wood or balsa, 3in. wide by 12in. long and ½in. thick. Sandpaper the wood carefully. Next obtain a sheet of cork ¼in. thick, and cut two strips 12in. by 1in. Glue the two strips to the base board with the long edge of the cork lined along the side of the base board, leaving a groove in the centre. Weight the cork down until the glue is dry. Later, neatly paste lining paper over the two cork strips, making sure that it is smooth and not wrinkled.

Suitable Setting Boards

Width Base Board	Groove	Thickness Side Pieces
1in.	¼in.	¼in. Micro-moths and Pug Moths.
1¼in.	⅛in.	¼in. Medium-sized Blues.
2½in.	¼in.	¾in. Large moths and butterflies.

Setting needles. Setting needles are probably the most useful item of equipment in setting all insects. Therefore it is important that you should have a number of setting needles of varied size. To make handles, obtain several wooden meat skewers from your local butcher, drill a hole in one end of each and insert the eye end of a needle tipped with glue.

Pins. When you are pinning insects do not use household pins, as they corrode easily and damage the specimens. Write to a natural-history dealer, and ask for a sample card of entomological pins; these are usually coated with black enamel. You will find they are numbered, and you can order a quantity – a box of a quarter or half an ounce. Large butterflies and moths need a Size 16 pin, while the smaller Blue butterflies need a Size 7. For Pug Moths and the larger Micro-moths use a stainless steel Size 2 pin.

Tracing paper or dry mounting tissue. Tracing paper or dry mounting tissue is used in setting the insect, to hold the wings in position until they are dried. Cut the sheet into strips 1½in. wide, and as long as you like, then put them on one side for future use.

Data labels. These are essential, for, as you will have realized from previous chapters, no specimen is of any scientific value unless it has full data. To save time when setting the insect, have a number of labels ready cut and available for use. You can keep them handy in a matchbox or small container. Cut them all to one standard size, so that there is uniformity in your specimens when they are finally pinned in your collection. A useful size is a label measuring ½in. by ¾in., either of white paper or thin card.

Setting

With a suitably sized setting board and your setting equipment on the table in front of you, you can start work. But first of all make sure you are quite comfortable and have a good working light.

Take out the first papered specimen and check the number and the data written on the flap with the notes and number entered in your field note-book. Make sure that the insect is perfectly relaxed. Take a small data label and carefully, with a mapping pen, in small neat printing in Indian ink, print the date on which the specimen was taken, the locality – as detailed as possible – and your own name. Carefully pin this label on the setting board so that it does not get lost.

Unfold the paper, and with a setting needle, ease the specimen onto the table. Gently pick up the insect from below, between the thumb and forefinger of the left hand, while with your right hand holding the entomological forceps, pick up a suitably sized pin.

Ease the pin through the centre of the thorax, and push gently down and through the body to a position three-quarters of the way up the pin.

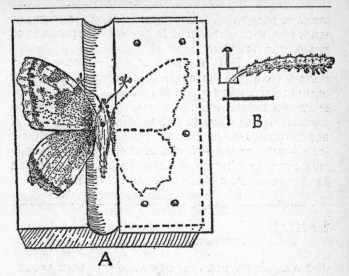

A. Showing butterfly on setting board with the left wing set and pinned in position

B. Caterpillar mounted on straw and set in balsa. Pin holds specimen and data label in position

Holding by the pin, gently lower it into the groove and press the pin home. With the setting needle and pressing dorsally behind the pin, ease the head, thorax and abdomen down into the groove.

Secure the abdomen firmly by pinning on either side.

Cut a piece 3in. long from the strip of tracing paper, and have it close to your left hand. With the setting pin in your right hand gently press the fore and hind wings on the left-hand side of the specimen flat against the setting board.

Still holding the wings flat, with the setting needle in your right hand, pick up in your left hand the strip of tracing paper. Lay the strip over the wing and in line with the edge of the setting board, holding it in position with the index finger and thumb with just sufficient pressure to hold the wing in position.

With the setting needle in the right hand, arrange the wing

in its setting position. In a well-set specimen, the hind margin of the fore wing should be at right angles to the long axis of the body. The hind margin of the fore wing should only slightly overlap the hind wing.

When the wing is in the correct position, with the forceps in your right hand, pick up a pin and press it home in place of the index finger, a second in place of the thumb, and a third at the point where the fore wing and hind wing overlap and slightly to the side.

Repeat this procedure for the right wing, placing the data label underneath the strip and just below the right hind wing.

With a fine setting needle, place the antennae in position and fix with crossed pins; with moths set the fore and hind legs.

Examine the specimen carefully, making sure the hind margins of the fore wings are at right angles to the long axis of the body and no part has slipped.

Having set the first specimen, carry on until you have completed the day's catch. Then place the specimens in a warm, dust-free cupboard to dry. Insects should not be removed from the setting board until they are perfectly dry, and this will depend largely on the weather and the time of year. Normally two to three weeks will be sufficient, but before removing the specimens, press the abdomen gently with the setting needle. If it is quite hard, then the insect can be safely removed from the setting board and the data label affixed to the pin. The specimen is then ready for final recording and storage.

Final recording

Using the index card 5in. by 3in., headed with the species, drawer or storage-box number, and rules into seven columns, copy the details of capture from the field note-book on to the card. The number in column 1 is the number of the insect of that species in your collection. Enter the specimen number clearly on the corner of the data labels. The specimen is then ready for storage.

Storage

Collections can be housed in one of two ways, either in a cabinet or a store box. Cabinets, though expensive, are ideal, but normally beyond the pocket of the young naturalist – that is, unless they can be purchased cheaply at a sale. Store boxes, on the other hand, can be bought from natural-history dealers. They have three advantages over the cabinet – more boxes can be added as you require them, they are readily portable, and they can be kept like books in a bookcase. Store boxes are available in three sizes, but I would recommend you make or purchase one 17½in. by 12in. (outside measurements). This will allow you ample room for your specimens, and you can house a reasonable number to a box.

You will be wise to examine the collections of butterflies and moths in your local museum before arranging your own. Notice that the specimens are arranged scientifically under Family, Genus and Species. To assist you with your own labelling you can purchase a printed 'label list' arranged in scientific order and ready for cutting up to pin in the collection. The store box should be ruled into suitable columns according to the size of your specimens, and the insects pinned between the pencil lines. The usual order of pinning your butterflies and moths is, typical male and female, a specimen mounted to show the underside uppermost, and a male or female mounted on its side. Room should be left for the inclusion of mounted ova, larvae and pupae, between the specimen and the printed-name label.

As the collection grows beyond one store box, you will need to think carefully about the organization and lay-out of your specimens. Each store box should be carefully labelled on the outside.

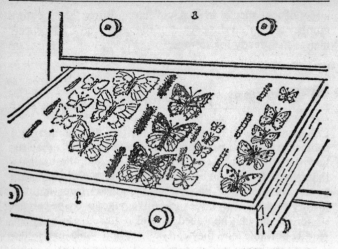

Butterflies and larvae arranged in cabinet

After placing your mounted specimens in the collection, and before you close the store box and put it away, look in the camphor cell and see if there is sufficient flake naphthalene (obtainable from chemists) to keep the box disinfected, and to prevent mites and beetles from attacking the specimens. Refill the camphor cell as often as necessary, and while you are doing this examine the specimens to ensure they are free from mites. The danger signs are particles of brown dust underneath the specimen.

When you put your store box away, ensure that it is never against an outside wall, nor in a room that is known to be damp. The most suitable position is raised off the ground in a warm, dry room.

Relaxing

There are times when it is impossible for you to set your specimens while they are still fresh and pliable, and after a few days they become hard and brittle. Before attempting to mount the insects in this condition, it is necessary to restore moisture to the body, so that it becomes supple. This process is known as 'relaxing'. There is one danger in this process that the young naturalist must guard against, namely mildew, particularly when water is the principal relaxing agent.

There are two methods of relaxing that the young naturalist might care to use and which are described in the next two paragraphs.

Procure a zinc or plastic box, three inches deep, with a tight-fitting lid. Mix sufficient plaster of Paris to cover the bottom of the box to the depth of one inch. When mixing the plaster add one or two drops of Lysol. When the plaster has set, cover the surface with a layer of blotting paper, then a very thin layer of cotton wool. Place your specimens on the cotton wool, shut the box lightly and leave for 24 hours, after which the specimen should be ready for setting. The cotton wool and blotting paper can be thrown away. Whenever you use the box, thoroughly wet the plaster with water and add a drop or two of Lysol. Use fresh blotting paper and cotton wool with every batch of specimens.

A second method of relaxing is to obtain a jar with a tight screw-top lid. Collect leaves of the cherry laurel and thoroughly bruise them with a mallet, after which the laurel should be pressed down in the jar and a piece of blotting paper laid on top. Place the specimen on the blotting paper and after 24 hours it should be relaxed and ready for setting.

Collection and preservation of ova

Where to look
Eggs are deposited by the imago on, or in the vicinity of, the food plant, though certain species drop their eggs while in flight, but only over ground on which the food plant is growing.

When searching for eggs you must carefully examine the upper and under side of each leaf as well as the plant stalk.

A useful aid in this quest is a low-powered magnifying glass. Other places that should not be neglected in your search are the buds and terminal shoots, the petals and ovary of flowering plants, and the axil of the sheath round the stem of grass plants. Collect the ova in a pill box.

Preservation
Method 1: Submerge the ova in hot, not boiling, water for two to three minutes. Dry on blotting paper, mount on a suitable sized coloured card and pin in the store box.

Method 2: Collect ova, prick each egg with a fine needle, and blow out contents with a very fine glass blowpipe. Work of this nature needs the use of a mounted lens. Mount the ova on a suitable coloured card or on a dried leaf or stem of the food plant and pin in the store box.

Method 3: Collect, and mount on a glass microscope slide, using gelatine as the fixative. Store in a tube containing 70 per cent alcohol with five drops of glycerine added.

Collection and preservation of larvae

Where to look
Larvae are collected on, or within the vicinity of, the food plant. When searching for caterpillars look for the tell-tale signs: eaten leaves, folded or spun leaves, sickly looking plants (stem- or root-feeding larvae), distorted flowers or buds, fruits or seeds which fall before they are ripe, silk threads, webs and a number of tits feeding. All are indications of the larvae that the young lepidopterist should not overlook. Collect the specimens in pill boxes, not forgetting to put a sprig of the food plant in with the larvae.

Preservation
When you get the larvae home, leave for 24 hours without food, then kill them in the ethyl acetate killing jar.

Place the caterpillar between two layers of blotting paper.

Using a pencil as a roller, place it just to the rear of the caterpillar. Should there be any difficulty, you can make a short cut in the area of the rear legs. Cut the internal organs free from the body, leaving the larval skin ready for drying.

The purpose of the method used is to keep the skin inflated while it slowly dries. In this manner the inflated skin will represent the living larvae. To this end, obtain a glass medicine dropper and remove the rubber teat, attaching in its place a piece of rubber tubing. Fasten the caterpillar to the glass medicine dropper by inserting the dropper end into the oval orifice (between the two rear feet), and holding it in position by means of a spring clip. At the other end of the rubber tubing attach the inside bladder of your football – blown up so that the air inside the bladder passes through the tube into the caterpillar skin, and keeps it fully extended to its natural size. Too much air will distort the specimen, so experiment until your specimen contains sufficient air to extend to its natural size.

Hold the specimen in front of a radiator, constantly turning it until the skin dries, when you should remove the caterpillar from the end of the dropper very carefully, as it will be quite brittle.

Mounting
There are three methods of mounting your specimens, either on wire, straw or alternatively on a piece of food plant. Pin a strip of paper with the full data written down, below the specimen.

Wind a length of silk-covered copper wire round a suitable entomological pin, leaving sufficient wire free on which to mount the specimen. Cover the wire with glue and press the specimen lightly on the wire, resting the length of the body between the prolegs and legs.

Gently ease a length of fine straw or a quill, lightly coated with glue, into the inflated skin, passing almost to the head. Pin through the straw and fasten in the store box.

Many collectors prefer to mount their specimens directly on to a dried part of the food plant.

Collection and preservation of pupae

Where to look
The pupae of Lepidoptera are generally very dull in comparison to the colourful imagos. There are exceptions, however, particularly among butterflies. To complete your collection you should try to mount at least one pupa for every series. Many pupae will be found attached to the food plant, either hanging by a thread or bound by a girdle. To find pupae you will have to search diligently, particularly on railings, fences, the leaves of trees, under loose bark and moss on the tree trunks, in the earth by the roots of trees and among herbage.

Killing
Method 1: Drop the pupae into boiling water for a few seconds. The surface of the pupae can be spirit varnished to replace the gloss lost in boiling water.

Method 2: For those specimens encased in a silken cocoon, the usual method is to inject with Carnoy's Fluid. This fluid can be made up at the chemists to the following formula:

Glacial acetate acid	...	..	5 MI
Alcohol 95 per cent	..	..	30 MI
Chloroform	...	...	15 MI

Mounting
Attach to a suitably sized coloured card and pin next to the larvae in the store box. Enter data on the underside of the card.

BEETLES

Although beetles form by far the largest Order of insects they can be recognized by the fore wings which, through

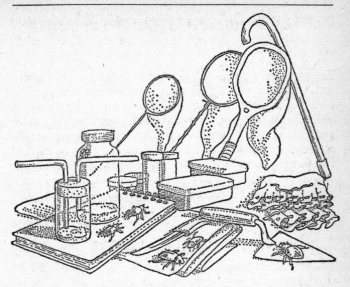

Collecting equipment for beetles

evolution, have become modified into *elytra*, or hard cases that serve to cover the delicately folded hind wings when the insect is not flying.

The beetle undergoes a complete *metamorphosis*, from ovum through the larval stage to pupa, and after a varying period emerging as the imago. The period of development from ovum to imago may take one month, or perhaps as long as three years.

Local knowledge

The collector of beetles, or coleopterist, should familiarize himself with the district in which he intends to collect, and, like the lepidopterist, should take every opportunity of using the sources of information available through the museum, natural history societies and local records (see pages 57–58).

You will find, as your interest in beetles develops, that you can collect at any time of the year, provided you know where to look.

Before you start collecting, find out as much as you can about the life history of each kind of beetle you require for your collection. Reference works will tell you the time of year and the time of day it is active, its food, and where on the food plant it is found. Look through the local records of Coleoptera to see if the species occurs in your district – if it does, find out where exactly it has been previously collected.

Armed with the information outlined above, the young naturalist should prospect the locality, making up his mind as to the most likely spot to find the insect.

Suitable collecting situations

Spring

Ants' nests: these should be visited during early mornings, and stones in the vicinity of the nest lifted and carefully examined.

Water beetles: the majority are found in well-weeded shallow water.

Damp bird and mammal nests: broken open on sheet.

Moss: squeeze and examine on sheet.

Carrion traps: fish used as bait will attract many beetles.

Keepers' racks: corpses usually contain a succession of beetles.

Summer

Dead or dying trees: search by beating and cutting open.

Timber piles: examine during early morning.

Compost heaps: use trowel.

Dung: thrown into water, and beetles collected.

Damp hay: shake fork load over a white sheet of paper or shaking cloth.

Decaying seaweed: examine while still damp.

Town refuse: use trowel.
Burnt timber and fire ash.

Autumn
Fungi: pulled to pieces over sheet.
Bees', wasps' or hornets' nests: make sure nests are old.
Cellars: in cracks and behind loose plaster.

Winter
Flood refuse: see page 85, sieving.
Damp refuse from hayricks and straw stacks: sorted over
    sheet.
Moss: squeezed and examined over sheet.
Tussocks of coarse grass: dug out and shaken over sheet.
Bark: torn off.
Stems of dead plants: torn off.
Warehouses, corn stacks and granaries.

Recording methods

A card index is the most suitable method of recording, that
is, in addition to the field note-book and field log. The information is entered on the card as outlined on page 21.
Any specimen listed in the index can be referred back to
the field note-book or field log by reference to the date of
capture.

Collecting equipment

Note-book.
Nets – light, sweep and water.
Pooter.
Killing bottle.
Tubes, pill boxes and tobacco
    tins.

Shaking cloth.
Walking stick.
Bags.
Knife and trowel.

Most of the items listed above are described in detail on pages 59–62 with instructions for the young naturalist on how to construct them. One or two of the items, such as the pooter and shaking cloth, may be new to you.

Pooter or aspirator. After the collecting tube or pill box, these are the most useful items of collecting equipment, and every young naturalist should possess one. They are simple

Using a pooter or aspirator

to make, and relatively inexpensive to purchase. They are used to capture small insects by suction, so saving handling and damaging delicate specimens. As you will see from the illustration above, the construction is simple – a small collecting bottle with a tight-fitting rubber bung or cork. A twist drill can be used, but a cork borer is preferable.

Two L-shaped lengths of glass tubing should be pressed through the cork – one to within 1½in. of the bottom of the bottle, and the second just one inch below the neck of the bottle. When you are pressing the tubing through the cork, make sure that the holes are sufficiently large to comfortably take the tubing and yet be air-tight. Fasten muslin over the end of the shorter piece of tubing at the inner end, while the outer end of the tube is fitted with a length of rubber tubing.

By placing the open end of the glass tubing over or near an insect, and sucking on the rubber tubing, you can draw small insects into the bottle. The pooter can be used for quickly collecting from the two nets, or from the ground, trunks of trees and walls.

The wise coleopterist always drops a plug of cotton wool inside the pooter and adds two drops of chloroform. This dopes the insects and prevents them from fighting each other. The insects can then be transferred from the pooter to the collecting tubes and pill boxes.

Shaking cloth. This is made from a light-coloured, durable cloth and measures 3 feet by 3 feet. It is invaluable when sorting herbage or moss, as the insects show up well against the light background, and can be quickly picked up with the pooter or tube. The shaking cloth is also useful spread under small bushes when beating with the walking stick, or while sorting out the catch from your nets.

Tubes and pill boxes. The most useful tubes for bringing specimens home alive are flat-bottomed tubes 3in. by 1in. These should contain a piece of tissue paper or muslin, to allow the insects to climb around without damaging or eating each other. Number each tube carefully by sticking on a paper label or piece of sticking plaster, on which a number can be written. This number is important when making notes in your field note-book.

Bags. These are used to bring home flood refuse, moss or fallen leaves that you wish to search at your leisure, or by using the berlese funnel (see page 85). The bags can be made from small flour sacks with a tape sewn round the top for tying.

Knife and trowel. Useful when pulling bark from tree

stumps and excavating among rubble, soil or straw in search of insects.

Collecting

Patience is a necessity in entomology. To collect unusual and rare specimens, the young naturalist must be prepared for a long and occasionally tedious search. You must never be disheartened if at the end of a long day you arrive home without the beetles you hoped to find. In any case, you will have made a number of captures that will fill gaps in your collection.

Beetles can be caught in a pill box or tube, pooter, net in flight or by sweeping. Whatever the method you use to capture the insect, transfer it carefully into a glass or plastic tube. Small beetles can be taken from the sweep or flight net with the pooter. At this point the young naturalist should number the tube or pill box, and make a full entry in his field note-book. The information should be laid out as follows:

Tube number.
Number of specimens.
Common or scientific name,
  if known.

Locality.
Detailed description of
  site of capture.
Other notes.

As a general rule young naturalists who collect Lepidoptera kill their specimens in the field. It is necessary to do this with butterflies and moths, otherwise they will get damaged, losing scales, antennae and even limbs before you get them home. Generally speaking, most coleopterists bring their specimens home alive, and kill them in their studies at their leisure. This allows them, as it will allow you, the opportunity to observe interesting specimens and make notes on their behaviour. Most of the insects in this Order are surprisingly tough, and would last a journey home tubed in your haversack without any damage; that is, if you have placed some tissue paper or muslin in the tube for the insect to cling to. Flies and other winged creatures should be killed in the field, otherwise they may damage their wings in transit.

Sweeping in thick herbage

Other methods of collecting

The beating tray

If you hold an open umbrella, ferrule downwards, under a bush or tree, then give the plant a sharp knock with a walking stick, you will find that a great number of insects will fall into the umbrella and can be examined for the specimens that you require. Although some entomologists use an umbrella to collect the falling insects while they are beating, you will find that this method has a number of disadvantages. The first is that the umbrella is not sufficiently shallow. Secondly, the spokes get in your way while collecting the insects. A simple beating tray can be made from a piece of black material, 1 yard square, and three strips of wood, 3 feet long, ¼in. thick and 1in. wide. Sew pockets on each of the four corners of the black material to strengthen it, and to serve to hold the ends of the strips of wood. Find the centre of two of the three strips of wood, and with a drill

Beating tray in use

bore a hole ¼in. wide through both of them; do the same at one end of the third strip of wood. Press a bolt through the two 3-foot struts which cross each other centrally and also through the hole of the third piece. This is to serve as a handle for the beating tray. Tighten the nut underneath, and you will have a shallow beating tray with a suitable handle that can be held under any bush or tree for beating, and into which the insects will fall; they can easily be seen against the black material and quickly picked up in the pooter or in the collecting tube.

Sieves
These are indispensable to the coleopterist, both at home and in the field; they are used for sieving drift material, foodstuffs and even the soil in search of insects. They can be made at home by soldering gauze or perforated zinc to a wooden or metal frame. The young naturalist should make one by cutting the bottom out of a fruit or toffee tin, and soldering wire gauze on. The tin should not be too deep, $1\frac{1}{2}$in. to 2in. is quite sufficient, and the smaller the sieve the more portable it is while in the field. It is possible to make a number of sieves, one fitting inside the other in nest fashion. These can be made at home from a different variety of tins; the largest should be 6in. in diameter, and the smallest 4in. in diameter. Each of the nested tins should have a mesh of a different gauge. The largest mesh should be on the smallest tin, and 3 or 4 mesh is most suitable. The second should be in 10 mesh, and the third in 24 mesh.

The berlese funnel
Many insects are difficult to extract from flood litter, grain and soil. The berlese funnel has been devised to drive insects from damp, dark refuse. A berlese funnel can be formed from a metal cone-shaped base with gauze or perforated zinc soldered on the top, and the bottom dipping into a tube of spirit. A 15-watt light bulb dries out the debris, the insects gradually move downwards to remain in the condition they like, until they fall down the funnel into the bottle of spirit below. The drying process should be slow, and each sample treated should take 3 to 4 days.

Mounting equipment

Entomological forceps.
Setting needles.
Mounting gum.
Pins.
Mounting cards.
Fine-hair paint brushes.
Labels.

Most of the equipment used in mounting beetles is the same as that described for lepidoptera. Mounting gum, mounting card and fine-hair paint brushes need a word or so of explanation.

Mounting gum. Mounting gum is used to attach the insect to the card. It should be colourless, should dry without leaving any mark on the mounting card, and should not dry too quickly or it will not give you time to adjust the specimen. Gloy, obtainable from most stationers, is very satisfactory, though care should be taken to see that the bottle is corked immediately after use.

Alternatively, the chemist will dispense the following gum for you:

10 grains Pulv gum Tragacanths.

30 min Sp Vini Meth.

Add sufficient water to make one ounce. These adhesives have the advantage in that they can be softened by moistening.

Some coleopterists use an adhesive made by dissolving celluloid in amyl acetate (not ethyl acetate, the killing agent). Place the celluloid, cut into small pieces, in a jar and add a little amyl acetate gradually; as the celluloid softens add more amyl acetate, stirring with a glass rod. When the adhesive is ready, it should be sufficiently thick to remain attached to the rod without running.

Mounting card. Although expensive, the best card on which to mount beetles is white Bristol board. It has a pleasing white polished surface and one board can be cut into a number of pieces of suitable size for mounting. The size of each piece will, of course, depend on the size of the insect. To save time, the young naturalist should have a number ready cut and stored in matchboxes; each box should be labelled with a specimen card glued on the outside. This will save you a great deal of time when mounting. The following sizes will cover your immediate needs: 9mm × 14mm, 17mm × 32mm, and 22mm × 40mm.

You should make sure that each small rectangle is evenly and cleanly cut. Nothing is worse in collections than to see badly cut and dirty mounting cards.

Brushes. You should have a number of brushes to use in spreading the adhesive on cards and brushing out the legs and antennae of beetles. Make sure you have a varied range of sizes.

Mounting

There are three methods of mounting beetles, each of which have their advantages. The young naturalist will have to decide which method is most suited to his needs.

Direct pinning. By this method a long entomological pin is passed directly through the body of the beetle until $\frac{1}{4}$in. is left showing above the insect. The pin should be inserted

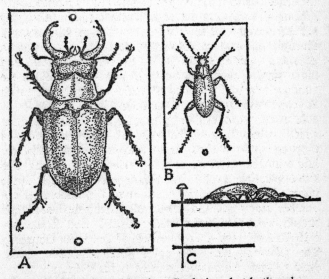

A. Large mounted beetle.   Card pinned at both ends
B. Smaller beetle.   Card pinned at one end only
C. Mounted beetle and data label

through the right wing case (elytron) of the insect, and never through the centre as with butterflies and moths.

Press the pinned insect into a sheet of thick cork until the legs are resting on the cork. Arrange the legs and antennae with the setting needle and fix in position with pins.

Prepare a data label, obtaining the essential information from your field note-book.

Example – Locality. (Town or country.)
Detailed locality – area.
Habitat.
Date.
Collector.

Pin the data label near the specimen and set aside to dry. When dry, remove the pins holding the legs and antennae in position. Push the specimen pin through the label and place the beetle in your store box or cabinet.

Carding. Choose a card of suitable size from those already prepared on which to mount your specimen.

Place the specimen on its back and brush out the limbs and antennae into the setting position.

Place a small blob of adhesive centrally on the card. With the forceps lift the specimen gently, turn it over and place it on the adhesive. Adjust the specimen with the setting needle, then allow the specimen to stand for half an hour until the adhesive dries.

With a dry brush and the setting needle, place the legs and antennae in position ready for fixing. Taking a little adhesive on your brush, paste it under each leg and the antennae; then give a final adjustment with the setting needle.

Push a pin through the card, prepare the data label and set the specimen aside in a dirt-free cupboard until dry.

Thread the data label on the pin and place the specimen in collection. Certain entomologists cover the card with adhesive before setting the specimen, though I would not advise you to do this, though it is an easier method, as the adhesive may discolour and spoil the mounting.

A second method of carding beetles is sometimes used by

entomologists (see illustration below). The insect is mounted on the tip of a triangular piece of Bristol board with a 10-mm base and 15-mm sides. Adhesive is placed on the tip, and the insect mounted on it. The advantage of this method is that it allows you the opportunity of examining the underside or ventral surface of the insect, though the method has three disadvantages: the legs and antennae are

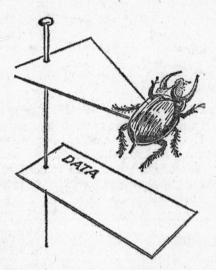

easily broken off; the insect has a tendency to spring loose from the mount if moved often; and, lastly, it does not look attractive in the store box.

Should you ever wish to mount a small beetle so that it can be removed for examination, a method has been devised called *staging* (see illustration on page 90). By this means the insect is pinned, using a stainless steel headless pin, by the method described on page 87 under direct pinning. The stage is made from polyporus, the bracket fungus found attached to trees. Normally it can be bought ready cut from a dealer quite cheaply in small quantities. It is supplied in 3-in. strips, and these can be cut to the required size. Cork, pith

or balsa wood can be used as an alternative to polyporus. The pinned insect is picked up by the forceps and attached to the stage. The data label is added underneath and the specimen is ready for the collection.

Footnote. Soft-bodied insects, such as moths or bugs, can be mounted using the staging method. The pins to use in this instance are black steel pins.

Recording

Before the insect is stored, the young naturalist should bring his records up to date. Recording Coleoptera is best done on 5in. by 3in. index cards, one card to every specimen. To catalogue your collection accurately you will need *A Catalogue of British Coleoptera*; this can be readily purchased from a dealer. As you glance through this catalogue you will notice that it is arranged scientifically, very much as your specimens are arranged in the store boxes, and, secondly, that each specimen has a number from 1 to 3,566. Carry out the following procedure:

Enter the catalogue number of the insect you are recording in the top left-hand corner of the index card, and after it the letter A, to signify that this is the first insect of that species in your collection. When you capture a second, use the letter B. For a third, the letter C, and so on.

Write the common and scientific names of the insect in the top right-hand corner of the index card.

Copy the notes from your field note-book on to the index card – date, locality, detailed locality, habitat and full conditions of capture, and any such information as you feel necessary.

Enter the same number, neatly, on the corner of the data label attached to the specimen by the pin.

Storage

After filing the index card, the beetles are ready to be stored. Beetles are stored in the same way as butterflies and moths, so re-read pages 71–2 carefully. You should examine your collection regularly. Additional precautions can be taken

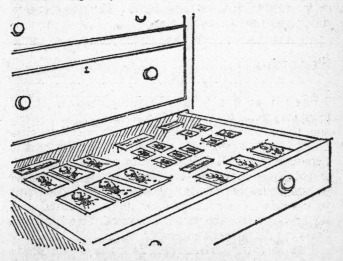

Beetles arranged in cabinet

by soaking small wads of cotton wool or sponge in beech-wood creosote and pushing them up to the head of long pins. A piece of thick cardboard should be placed below each pin to prevent the creosote dropping on the base of the store box and staining it.

OTHER TYPES OF INSECTS

Order – Orthoptera – grasshoppers; locusts; crickets; cockroaches

Preservation
Leave for 24 hours without food. Kill with ethyl acetate or benzole vapour, a few drops on cotton wool.

With a fine-pointed pair of scissors carefully cut along abdomen up underside or ventral surface. Clean out body cavity with fine-pointed forceps and cotton wool. Gently rub in borax and glycerine. Prepare a sliver of wood wrapped and coated with borax and glycerine and insert in the abdomen.

Mount on card or celluloid as illustrated on page 87.

Order – Dermaptera – earwigs

Collecting
Found hiding under stones, bark and leaves. Has a particular liking for flowers and can be found among the petals.

Preservation
Kill by using ethyl acetate or benzole vapour, and mount on card. Strap the abdomen down to prevent curling during drying.

Order – Plecoptera and Ephemeroptera
– stone-flies and mayflies

Collecting
Among stones near water, or taken by sweeping waterside
vegetation.

Preservation
Kill by using laurel leaves or strong ammonia fumes. Mount
using a setting board as in Lepidoptera, bracing the wings,
abdomen and legs with paper and pins. Alternatively, the
insects can be mounted directly on card, setting the wings
and other parts with a liquid paste.

Order – Hemiptera – (Heteroptera)

Collecting
Hemiptera can be successfully collected by all the methods
so far described, except netting. Examine bark and foliage,
using a pooter to pick up the specimens.

Preservation
Great care is needed in mounting, as the identification
characters are on the underside of the body.
    Kill by using ethyl acetate.
    Bend a card along its long axis, and pass a pin through
either end of the bent card. Remove the pin at the end that is
to hold the specimen.
    Pin the specimen, using a small headless pin, and passing
the pin through the scutellum of the insect from the underside while it is laid on its dorsal side.
    Holding the insect by the pin with the forceps, pass the
body of the pin through the holes prepared. The springiness
of the card will hold the pin in position.

Order – Odonata – dragonflies and damselflies

Collecting
Caught using net. It is advisable for you to wear wellingtons, as these insects fly over muddy water out of striking distance from the bank of stream or river.

Preservation
Leave without food for 2 to 3 days.
 Kill with ammonia, *not* ethyl acetate.
 Cut along abdomen. Carefully remove contents, taking care not to damage inner lining of abdomen.
 Prepare a sliver of wood, cotton wool covered, to fit in the abdomen, and cover with borax and glycerine and place in position.
 Push pin centrally through the thorax.
 Pin to setting board, and paper and pin wings, legs and abdomen as illustrated on page 69.

Order – Homoptera – aphids; whiteflies and scale insects

Collecting
May be picked off the plant with a pooter, or a brush dipped in spirit. Often the insects and the plant can be collected together, placed in an airtight tin and carried home.

Preservation
Carefully place insects in small corked tube containing 80 per cent alcohol.
 Data should be written on a slip of paper in pencil and inserted in the tube before corking. Enter a note on the data label as to the colour of the specimen.

Order – Neuroptera and Megaloptera – lacewings and alderflies

Collecting
By net or light trap. The young naturalist should be careful when handling these insects, as many can bite.

Preservation
Kill by using laurel leaves or chloroform.
   Card the specimen, fastening wings, antennae and legs with a little gum.

Order – Trichoptera – caddisflies

These are well known to the young naturalist in larvae form, with the larval cases constructed from sand grains, pebbles, twigs and leaves. The adult looks rather like a moth, but has hairy and not scaly wings.

Collecting
At night, in a light trap. During the day by sweeping or netting. Beat waterside herbage to disturb specimens.

Preservation
Kill by using ethyl acetate.
   Cover setting board with a sheet of cellophane, moulding it to the surface of the board with the fingers.
   Set the specimen using the method described for Lepidoptera, and pinning the fore and hind legs out.

Order – Diptera – true flies

(True fore wings, hind wings modified into knobbed organs called halteres.)

Collecting
All methods of collecting. It is effective to use the pooter when taking specimens out of the net.

Preservation
Kill by using ethyl acetate.

Mounting
Method 1: large specimens.
  Pin through thorax.
  Press pin into sheet of cork covered with clean paper.
  Arrange and pin wings (extended), and legs as in direct pinning (see page 87).
  When specimen is dry, stage on a card, fixing body, wings and legs with gum.
Method 2: small specimens.
Staged in polyporus. For details see page 89.
  An alternative method with small specimens is pointing (see page 89 for discussion of method).

Order – Hymenoptera – bees; wasps; ants; ichneumon flies

Collecting
By netting or stalking. Be careful when handling specimens, otherwise you might be stung. *Do not* try to collect bees and wasps from a nest unless you have an adult naturalist with you.

Preservation
Use ethyl acetate on all specimens.

Mounting
Method 1: large specimens.
  Pin through thorax and set wings, legs and antennae on setting board as for Lepidoptera.
Method 2: small specimens.
  Gum on side to a card, spreading out the wings, legs and antennae so that the abdomen is clearly visible.

9 WATCHING BIRDS

A glimpse of an unusual bird is sufficient to start the inquisitively minded boy or girl on the search for more information, and this in turn leads to the hobby of bird-watching. Bird-watching can be practised anywhere. Gardens, town parks, woodland, the seashore and cliffs, river estuaries, mountains and moorland all have birds of interest to the young bird-watcher. Even the most unlikely places will yield results to the observant boy or girl. London has a number of unusual if not rare birds in the city centre; sewage farms regularly attract birds to feed and rest; while slag heaps of industrial areas reveal many unusual and rare migrants.

You will not have to go far afield in search of interesting material. Watching the birds feeding at the bird table from your own window will give you an insight into bird behaviour; you will learn many facts, not only about the way birds feed, but also about their shape, the size of their bills and the colour of their plumage.

Binoculars

Binoculars are essential if you are going to study birds from a distance and to be able to jot down in your field notebook the identification characters. New binoculars are rather expensive to buy, though you may be fortunate enough to get a pair second-hand. Whether you buy them new or second-hand, you should always get the advice of an experienced adult naturalist, as many pairs of new binoculars sold on the market are entirely unsuitable for bird-watching, while second-hand ones may have damaged lenses. If you see an advertisement in a newspaper for binoculars, you should most certainly get advice before you write for them. Binoculars are an expensive item so you must take care to choose the most suitable glasses when you have the chance. When choosing, remember that the magnification should not be too great, otherwise you will have difficulty in keeping the glasses steady on the bird you are viewing. Light-gathering power is perhaps the most important point, and a suitable pair of binoculars are those marked 8×30. These figures give you in the case of the figure 8, the magnification, and in the case of the 30 the field of vision. A useful hint when buying glasses is that the magnification power should multiply into the figure for the field of vision approximately three times. Most glasses are bi-focal, which means that the focusing controls both eyepieces. Normally, there is a central screw that you can work with your right hand, while the glasses are held to your eyes. Individual focusing for each eyepiece is never satisfactory, as by the time you have adjusted both the bird will normally be out of the field of vision. Appendix F gives you the names and addresses of reputable firms making binoculars. Write for catalogues and you can choose the most suitable pair at your leisure. One last word – never be too hasty, for if you are you will be bound to regret it later. A word with a bird-watcher of long experience is invaluable when purchasing glasses.

Some bird-watchers use telescopes, but generally they are ornithologists who specialize in sea birds and wild fowl. It is important to remember that a telescope is very difficult to hold steady, and if you use one in the field, you need to take some form of tripod with you to obtain satisfactory results.

Reference works

You will need a suitable book on British birds, one that gives full details of the field characters, as well as possessing accurate illustrations. As with binoculars, the reference work must be carefully chosen. There are many which at first glance seem to be suitable, but on closer examination are not satisfactory for a field worker. Perhaps the ideal work is *The Handbook of British Birds* in five volumes. Although such a work may be beyond your pocket, except perhaps at Christmas or on your birthday, it can be readily consulted in the reference room at your public library. There is *A Field Guide to the Birds of Britain and Europe* by R. Peterson, G. Mountford and P. A. D. Hollom (Collins) which is moderately priced and contains a great deal of very useful detail, particularly on the field characters. Be very careful when you are purchasing a book, and never allow anyone to buy you a bird book without first consulting you. As with the binoculars, ask your local naturalist for advice, and he will suggest the right book for you to use. A list of reference works is given in Appendix B.

Recording

You will need your field note-book to make descriptions of birds you see, which you cannot recognize immediately. Quick sketches are invaluable and save a tremendous amount of the time normally taken writing descriptions out in long hand. The plumage colour and patterns, as well as the shape of the head, beak and feet can be marked easily on the drawing.

The drawing on page 100 is intended to guide you when sketching in the field. If you construct your birds on the same lines you will find that it is not as difficult as you may have thought. After a while you will become quite proficient and might attempt to copy your field sketches and colour them at home.

It is important that you should know, too, what is called the topography of a bird. That is the term used to describe the various parts of the body plumage. The drawing on this page shows these parts and the names that have been given to them. Using these in your field notes and on your drawings will save a great deal of time.

Notes taken in the field must be as accurate as possible; the following notes and points may aid you in making your observations.

Size

The size of a bird is important and should be jotted down in your field note-book. You may not be able to give an accurate measurement of the length of the body, but by comparing it with something you know well, you will have a reasonable idea in your own mind.

Shape

The shape of a bird is important as well, and it can be described as being long, thin and built on graceful lines, or plump and rounded.

Colour

Try, when noting the colour of a bird, to be as accurate as

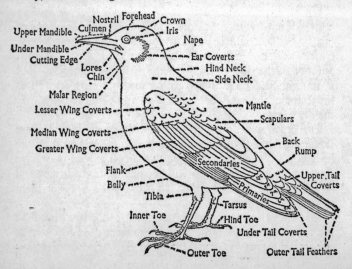

you possibly can. Nothing is more misleading than colour, particularly when you have to compare the notes you have made with illustrations in a reference work, where the colours are to a certain extent artificial. In flight, certain birds show colours which are not visible when resting. These colours and markings are important in identification, and should be noticed if possible and jotted down or sketched.

Movement
This is the way the bird behaves in flight. Notice whether the flight is straight and direct, or undulating; the height at which the bird flies from the ground; whether the wings move slowly or quickly; whether it glides or hovers.

Situation
When you notice a bird through your glasses, make a note in your field note-book of its habitat. This information may be useful when making an identification.

Song
Many bird-watchers can identify a bird from its song. This takes a great deal of practice and you will have to develop an ear for recognizing the songs. Invaluable aids to this method of recognition are the gramophone records of bird song made by Dr Ludwig Koch and Eric Simms. It is unwise to identify the bird from its song alone, until you become fairly proficient. At first you should see the bird, make a written description or sketch in your field note-book and then listen to its song. Alternatively, listen to the song, try to identify it and then wait until the bird becomes visible before you make a definite identification.

Observation in the field

Two locally common birds, the blackbird and the thrush, provide material for really intensive research by the young naturalist bird-watcher. Very little is known about the day-to-day activities of a nesting hen thrush, for instance. When does she start work? How many times does she rest? How much does she eat? How far does she travel away from the nest? How does she occupy herself while she is sitting? You will not find the answers to these and many other questions in text-books, but only by accurate observation. If your records are based on this form of field work, they will form a valuable part of ornithological knowledge.

Pairing and nesting
Notice where the birds fly to, and where they come from.

Do they return in the same direction, and if so, are they collecting nesting material?

If you see two birds together, are they rival cock birds ready to fight for a hen bird, or are they a pair?

If they are constructing a nest, what materials are they using?

If the bird is a cock bird, is it establishing a territory? (Most of our common birds feed every day over more or less the same ground, and if nesting in that area, will fight other birds off. Technically, this is called a territory.)

Establish where and when the bird started nesting, how many eggs there are, and when the first egg was laid. Great care must be taken in approaching the nest, and the bird must never, under any circumstances, be disturbed or frightened.

Watch the nest carefully, and note whether it is the male or the female that sits on the eggs (in many species both sexes sit on the eggs, in others the female does this, while the male sings to and feeds her).

If it is the female returning to the nest, does she turn the eggs, or clean and tidy the nest? What is the male doing? If he is feeding, how often does he come with food? What is the food?

Note the date when the eggs hatch and the fledglings leave the nest.

Measuring bird flight
Birds travel tremendous distances. Swallows fly 6,000 miles from South Africa to Britain in spring, and return in winter. Redwings leave Scandinavia in the autumn, and winter in Britain. Although the young bird-watcher cannot attempt to measure the swallow's daily flights on its migratory journey, he can measure flight while nest building is in progress. It has been calculated that a pair of long-tailed tits travelled 600 miles while collecting feathers for their nest. It is difficult to expect you to make observations of this order, but you can, by careful watching, work out the number of flights made by a bird during the building of its nest, or while feeding, in one hour of observation. Establish what nesting or feeding material is being used, and the distance of the nest from the site where it is being obtained. Then count the number of journeys the bird makes. The number of journeys multiplied by the distance will give you an approximate figure.

Migration
The young naturalist can make a number of observations on migrating birds. In spring, he can record his first sighting of such birds as the swallow, swift and cuckoo, as well as the date of their departure. Similarly, the arrival of the winter migrants can be noted.

Dead birds

When you visit your local museum, examine the mounted specimens carefully, or, better still, examine the collection of cabinet skins if these are available, and notice details of plumage of the birds particularly the colours. Try to find out the difference in plumage between the young or juvenile birds, an adult cock bird and an adult hen. You will be surprised at the variations in plumage colour in certain species, and these can prove very deceptive when you are in the field. The more you can examine birds in your hand or behind glass in your local museum, the better bird-watcher you will be. Familiarize yourself with as many of the British birds as you can in this way.

You may have the opportunity of forming your own collection at home, provided your mother and father are willing to cooperate with you. Mounted birds can be bought quite cheaply at sales, or you may find them among junk in old attics, or be given them by a friend who wants to get rid of them. Take them out of their cases and store them in cellophane envelopes. In this way they take up less room, can be stored in drawers, and probably cause less trouble than they would if they were in old-fashioned large cases or cabinets. Birds such as these are ideally suitable for comparison with descriptions in reference books, drawings and coloured illustrations. There is one point, however, that you should bear in mind, old birds may have been in the sun and consequently their plumage will have faded slightly. Nevertheless, they are still quite valuable.

You may like to do a little taxidermy on your own, that is, to make up a collection of bird skins for yourself. This is not difficult, provided again you have the cooperation of your mother and father, and that you yourself have the time and enthusiasm to practise. Your first cabinet skin will not be a success, and until you are experienced you will not make a skin that is as neat and tidy as those which you might have seen in your local museum.

What is the difference between a mounted specimen and a cabinet skin? The first is an exhibition specimen, such as the ones you see in your museum, where the taxidermist has tried to re-create the dead bird in a life-like position. A cabinet skin, on the other hand, is made to the shape of a very fat cigar, not mounted at all. The purpose of the cabinet skin is to make a specimen that is readily available for study, easy to handle and does not take up too much storage space.

Material for your skin collection may be obtained on your bird-watching expeditions. You will, from time to time, come across bird casualties. This is regrettable, but is unavoidable; severe winters, lack of food, careless motorists all take their toll of bird life. Pass the word round to your friends that you would be grateful if they would let you have any dead birds that they find.

Making a cabinet skin

Equipment
The equipment you will need to make your cabinet skin is not expensive.

A good scalpel. (Preferably a Swan Morton, with replaceable blades. These can be purchased from your local surgical dealer or from a chemist; if they are not readily available, they can be ordered.)

A pair of pointed scissors.

Forceps.

Light magnesium carbonate. This is obtainable from your chemist and is used to absorb body liquids while you are skinning. Such liquids tend to spoil the feathers if they are allowed to run.

Borax. This is used to preserve the skin. It is a commercial product and can again be obtained from the chemist.

Cotton wool.

Small slivers of wood of varying size.

Preliminary examination
Note down on a piece of paper the locality where the bird was found.

Note down the colour of the soft parts of the bird's body and of the beak, feet and eyes.

Jot down notes on the colour and markings of the plumage.

Measurements
You will need a ruler marked in millimetres and a pair of dividers. All measurements of birds should be given in millimetres.

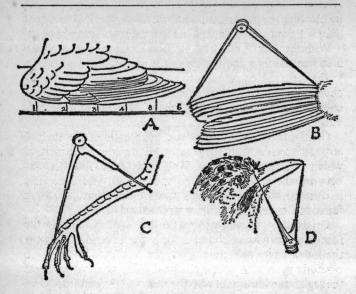

Wing: press the wing on the ruler until it is quite flat. Thus you will obtain the longest measurement from the carpel joint to the tip of the longest feather. This is known as the wing length (see illustration A above).

Tail: this is measured with the dividers by placing one divider tip to the skin between the tail feathers and opening the dividers until the other tip touches the longest part of the tail feathers (see illustration B).

Beak: place one tip of the dividers at the base of the beak against the skull, the other tip at the point. The distance between is the bill length (see illustration D).

Tarsus: the measurement is taken as in illustration C.

Skinning

Place the bird before you resting on its back, tail pointing towards you.

With the fingers and scalpel handle separate the feathers on the abdomen. If the bird is a small one, this can be done by blowing, or damping the handle of the scalpel and running it through the feathers, curling them to either side.

With the scalpel, make an incision along the run of separated feathers from the bottom of the breast bone right down to the vent, taking care not to cut through the skin into the abdomen. If you do, sprinkle light magnesium carbonate over the incision and this will absorb the liquids that ooze out.

Gently, using your fingers and the handle of the scalpel, separate the skin from the flesh on either side of the incision which you have just made. Work gently, holding the skin between the index finger and the thumb, and loosening underneath with the handle of your scalpel. Continue this as far round to the backbone as you possibly can.

Gradually, you will expose the knee joints. Taking the foot in your right hand and holding the knee joint between the index finger and thumb of your left hand, slowly and carefully push with your right hand. The skin will slide off the leg as the knee joint and the flesh are pushed into view.

Cut entirely through this joint with the scissors, then grasping the end of the free bone with the index finger and thumb of your left hand, gradually pull the skin down as far as the ankle joint.

At this point you can clean all possible flesh off the leg itself.

When this has been done to both legs, press away the skin on either side of the rump, and with the point of the scissors cut through the vertebrae or backbone near the end, severing the tail stump entirely from the body. Be very careful at this point not to cut through the tail feathers, otherwise they will fall out. During the whole of this skinning, use your light magnesium carbonate freely to absorb the abdominal juices.

Stand the bird up on its head, and, using the fingers of both hands, ease the skin away from the body, working with the finger-nails and scalpel.

Sever the wings as you did the legs, and continue your skinning down to the neck and head.

When the base of the skull is reached, snip off the body

with a pair of strong scissors and lay it on one side.

With the thumbs of both hands, gently press the skin back over the skull until the ears are reached. The skin of the ears is deeply rooted in the skull, so with the tip of your scissors gradually work back the skin out of the cavities.

The eyes are next reached. Very great care must be taken here to avoid puncturing the lids or cutting the eyeballs. The eyeballs are filled with fluid, and if this is allowed to escape it will badly disfigure the feathers of the head. Skin down to the base of the beak.

With the scissors cut out a V at the base of the skull. Scrape out the brain of the bird, and remove the tongue with the scalpel or forceps.

With the skin inside out, you should clean all the meat from the skin. Make sure the meat has been completely removed from the leg bones, wing bones and tail stump. The interior of the skull should be thoroughly cleaned as well as the exterior. It is at this point that you must have the utmost patience. Go over the body of the bird, cleaning it several times until you are sure that no particle of flesh remains. When this has been done the skin is ready for poisoning.

Pour the commercial borax liberally over the skin, and rub well in with the fingers. Do not worry if the borax gets into the feathers; it will not harm them, and can be brushed out quite easily afterwards. When you have thoroughly poisoned the skin and made sure the borax has reached every part, you are ready for making.

Turn the skin the right way out and shake it until the feathers fall into place. Take a small piece of cotton wool with the forceps and push it up through the base of the skull into the eye-sockets on either side. This will fill the eye-sockets out, and with a little adjustment can be made to appear through the eye openings.

Take a sliver of wood an inch to two inches longer than the body, and, with the scalpel, gently nick the stick all the way along until it looks rather like a miniature Christmas tree. Taking some cotton wool, thin it out until you have just sufficient and feed it slowly on to the stick, turning the stick in your right hand, feeding the cotton wool with your left hand and turning the stick all the time. Gradually the cotton wool will build up on the stick and can be moulded with the hand until it is exactly the size of the body of the bird. Point the stick at the top and work it through the opening in the bird skin up to the skull and between the beak. Then adjust the skin round the false body.

Sew up the body, fasten the legs to the stick at the base which protrudes from the opening, and adjust the wings in their natural position, using cotton wrapped round the body to hold them. Tie the beak together with a piece of cotton.

Write out a small label with the following data and attach it to the legs, tying it to the specimen with a piece of cotton.

On one side of the label write:

Scientific and common name of the bird.

Locality where the bird was found and the date.

Name of finder.

Sex of the bird – and whether juvenile or adult.

On the second side of the label write:

Colour of the soft parts of the body.

Preservative used.

Name of taxidermist.

After the label is attached, the skin should be wrapped in cotton wool and put on one side to dry.

At first you will find that skinning is very tedious and difficult, but gradually, as you gain more experience, the process will speed up and as you become more proficient you should be able to turn out a neat cabinet skin in 20 minutes or less.

Partial preservation

The footprints of birds can be found on river banks, marshes, shore or estuaries. Provided the sand or soil is not too wet, plaster casts can be made of the footprints and coloured in the way described in Chapter X. If you search the mud surrounding the footprints very carefully, you will find that the bird has been feeding and that the feeding marks are visible. These can be sketched in your note-book and/or cast in plaster.

Birds' nests

Old nests can be collected and mounted. This provides a fascinating occupation after the nesting period and throughout the autumn. Study the construction of the nests and find out what materials were used during the process.

Bird pellets

Many birds cast up pellets of undigested parts of their food. The study of these will give you a great deal of information about the food of birds, and when they are mounted will provide you with material for display in your small museum. Many birds, including owls, crows, herons, fly-catchers and robins cast up pellets which can be collected in a matchbox and taken home. Soak the pellet in warm water for half an hour or so, and with the setting needle gently tease out the pieces. When they are dry these can be mounted on a sheet of card and named. You will be surprised at the things you will find: the hair and skin of mammals, feathers of birds, bones, the elytra of hard backs of insects, and so on.

Nesting boxes and bird tables

These can be constructed at home and put out in the garden. They will give a tremendous amount of pleasure, particularly if placed in front of, or near to, one of the house windows. In the case of nesting boxes they will be used by tits particularly. The food table will be used by birds of all kinds and you will be surprised at the number which come to feed; perhaps the lesser-spotted or greater-green woodpecker may be a frequent visitor if you live near woodland. Place the food and water regularly on your table and the birds will make a habit of coming, and soon be old friends.

You will find that the larger British mammals are easy to watch, provided you exercise a little care. Many towns have badger sets, fox earths or even otter holts on the outskirts, if not near the town centre, and if you can read the tracks and signs left by their occupants, you will know where to locate them. Deer can be found in many parks and they will provide you with a splendid opportunity for watching our largest wild land mammal.

Most of our larger British mammals have acute senses of

Badger watching

smell, hearing and sight; these are suited to their mode of life and they make excellent use of them in discovering any form of threatening danger. To watch any British mammal you must be a good woodsman, exceptionally patient, and ready to withstand a considerable amount of discomfort, particularly during the summer evenings when the midges are active.

Reconnoitre the animal hole a day or so before you intend to start your watch to make sure that the animals are using it and that there has been recent activity. Let the farmers or keepers know what you are doing and if they approve of you they will pass on valuable information. With the badger set, you must look for the latrines: see if they have been used recently; whether or not there are footprints in the wet mud or sand at the front of the entrance, and search carefully for badger hairs on surrounding bushes or the underside of fences. With the fox's earth, search for the remains of recent meals – chicken feathers, bones and animal fur. The most usual signs at the otter's holt are the footprints or 'seal' of the otter which you will find in the sand at the entrance. Smell is always a useful guide as to whether the animals are using their homes or not, particularly the pungent, musky smell of the fox.

On the day you are going to watch, arrive early (before dusk), and select your hiding-place in daylight in order to make sure that it is a good one, and to ensure that you have ample time to make yourself comfortable. Test the wind to make sure your scent is blown away from the entrance to the set or earth, and see that you are not on a skyline. If you are using a tree, either stand or sit in front of it with your back to the trunk, or climb up and watch from the branches above, provided they are safe and you are not likely to fall off at the critical moment.

Whenever the animal is within the vicinity you must keep perfectly still. Above everything you must not move if the badger or fox is actually out of its hole. The slightest noise will disturb it and, once it is frightened, there is no chance of the animal coming out again the same night.

S–F

The time when the animal will emerge from its hole is governed by the immediate environment. If animals are suspicious, they may not come out at all; or they may wait until it is quite late and very dark. Alternatively, there are sets and earths very near the centre of towns, where the animals are used to the noise of traffic, the voices of people and the lights of houses, and come out at fairly regular times each evening. You will probably find that your badger will emerge from his set at dusk, provided everything is normal. This means that you must be in position at least one hour before dusk, and be prepared for at least two hours of patient waiting.

The badger may give an indication that he is coming out; a sharp yelp, snort or snuffle may tell you that he is near the entrance. You should remain perfectly still, with your eyes fixed on the entrance to the set. Gradually his head will emerge and he will sniff the air for any scent of an enemy; he may then go back for a few minutes and then come out again. If after sniffing he does go back, do not be too worried; wait quietly; he will probably come out again within a few minutes and walk slowly from the entrance of the set towards the latrines or the surrounding vegetation. The boar usually comes out first, followed by the sow, and if you are lucky, and it is the right time of the year, you may even see the cubs.

The fox's earth is not difficult to find. It may be an old badger set or an enlarged rabbit hole which you will be able to watch with comfort from a fixed hide. You can construct the hide from hessian or canvas and old poles, but make sure it is in position several days before you attempt to use it. This gives the fox the opportunity of getting used to this new object in the vicinity of his earth. Observations can be carried out easily from a hide, and the gambols of young cubs with the reproving snaps of the vixen, or the home-coming of the dog fox, can be watched from day to day. Indeed, if you are a photographer you will be able to get some very good pictures of the day-to-day life of your particular fox family.

If you live in a hunting district you will probably know that during the breeding season, the master of foxhounds makes special earths in order that vixens may give birth to their cubs safely. A knowledge of these earths will give you ample opportunity for watching foxes.

Deer are particularly difficult to watch, and to stalk. Unless you are watching up-wind they can detect your scent from distances varying from a few yards to as much as two miles.

As you become experienced, you will find it is unsafe to pass within a mile of a herd if you are stalking down-wind. Often long walks will have to be made to get into the right position.

Binoculars or a telescope are ideal equipment for deer-watching, provided you are carefully camouflaged when you are using them so that the light does not reflect from the lenses and frighten the animals.

The otter's holt is usually located on the banks of streams or rivers, by the roots of one of the large alder or willow trees growing there. It can be located by keeping a sharp look-out for the seal or spraints. During the late spring you may be fortunate enough to glimpse the dog otter fishing, while the bitch is teaching the young to emulate their father. At play, the otters whistle to each other, while a whimper may be an indication to you that all is not well. If it is excited or alarmed, the otter will give a shrill bark, not unlike that of a puppy, and this may be varied with the whistling call.

After the young are able to swim, the dog otter leaves the family and goes off on his own. He will wend his way over considerable tracts of country even away from water, feeding on moles, small birds, beetles and grubs. He travels by otter roads or defined pathways that only otters know, and spends his nights in holes in the hillsides or banks of streams, known as 'otter inns'.

You will find signs of otter along stony river banks, where the animal may select a flat-topped stone which it uses as a table and which is known to naturalists as an 'otter's altar'.

On this stone or round about it, there will be the remains of previous meals, the bones of fish or frogs, or even the bones and feathers of wild fowl.

The otter may be more difficult to locate and watch than either the badger or the fox; yet, when located it will provide you with a great amount of excitement as you watch the antics of the otter family during the warm spring evenings. You must be very wary in your movements, and extremely patient if you are going to be successful. Otters are notoriously careful animals and can so easily scent danger. Experience, however, will give you the practice you need in field craft and will enable you to be a successful watcher.

Always remember that observations made in the field and recorded in your field note-book are infinitely more valuable to you as a naturalist than the things that you read in textbooks.

Watching the smaller British mammals such as voles, shrews and mice will test your ingenuity as well as your patience.

There is a method which has been successfully used by a number of young naturalists with very good results, and which you might like to try out.

To find out where the small mammals are most active you will have to pre-bait an area for several nights. This is done by preparing the food for the animals from oatmeal, cooking fat and breadcrumbs. Boil up the fat and mix the oatmeal and breadcrumbs into it, then pour into small, shallow trays to cool. When the food is cool take it with you in your haversack, wrapped in paper, and place it along hedges, beside trees, and anywhere else you think these animals will be most active. Leave it overnight and return in the morning, carefully examining each food tray. It is easy to see if the animals have been feeding, as you will find part of the fat eaten, with the tooth or claw marks on the surface.

Pre-bait in this way for several nights and, when you are satisfied that the animals are visiting the food regularly, set up a small hide during the afternoon before the evening on which you are watching. As with the larger mammals, go down to the hide and make yourself comfortable an hour or so before dusk. Then sit patiently and wait until you hear noises coming from the undergrowth in the region of the food tray. When the animals are feeding, and certainly you will be able to hear them, take out a powerful torch, which you have previously covered with red cellophane, and shine it on to the food tray. A red light seems to have no effect on the animals and they will continue to feed while you are able to see them clearly in the light.

A continual watch of this sort will reveal most valuable information, which, if recorded in your field note-book, will be of very great use to naturalists.

Trapping mammals

You can make a great number of important observations, particularly on small mammals, by trapping them. Do not trap them in traps of the sort you see sold in ironmongers for rats and mice, but in specially prepared cages where the mammal is kept alive until you have examined it, ringed it and released it. A trap of this sort is not very expensive to purchase, but you can make one quite easily from a large sweet jar if you can persuade a confectioner to let you have one. Bury the sweet jar along one of the runs of the voles or mice. Camouflage it carefully, taking care to rub your hands well in the soil before you do so.

I must emphasize that trapping animals in this way should only be done when you can visit the traps regularly, preferably twice a day. The reason for this is that many animals are very prone to shock, and require a great deal of food to keep them alive. If they are left in a trap of this sort without food for more than several hours, they will die. You will have caused intense suffering and pain, and not behaved as a naturalist should. The best time to trap is during your school holidays, when you can visit the traps regularly, and release the animals immediately after you have examined them. Note the information in your field note-book.

From trapping of this kind, naturalists are able to plot the distribution of small mammals in an area, record the number of times they occur there, and note the territory or home range of the creatures.

DETAILED STUDY

There are many ways in which you can increase your knowledge of British mammals and your own museum collection. The following notes, although brief, will give you some indication of the things you can do.

Taking a plaster cast of an animal's footprint

Plaster casts of footprints

The footprints or the spoor of British mammals occur almost anywhere. You must search ditches, river banks, pathways, badger sets and fox's earths for likely prints to cast. When you have found a suitable set of footprints, choose the one that is most clearly defined. Clean it carefully, taking care not to disturb the footprint while brushing away any small stones, twigs or loose sand that may have fallen into the pad marks.

Bend a piece of tin round a jam jar, place it over the footprint and press it into position.

Empty some dental plaster of Paris into a mixing bowl and slowly pour in water, stirring all the time until the mixture both looks like and has the feel of cream. It is essential that there are no lumps or air bubbles in the mixture. Always stir following the wall of the mixing bowl.

Holding the tin frame, which you have placed over the footprint, with one hand, slowly pour in the plaster, using the tip of a knife to smooth the surface level.

Next take a piece of wire, bent to the shape of the letter U, push the loose ends into the plaster and leave the loop sticking out for about half an inch.

You should then leave the footprint to dry for a suitable period of time, depending on the weather. If it is humid, then the plaster will take longer to dry than on a normally fine or windy day.

When dry, lift the plaster cast and peel off the tin. Turn over, and you should have a perfect cast of the animal's footprint. Brush the loose earth from the cast and place it in cotton wool in a container. When you get the cast home and it has dried more thoroughly, you can place it in a drawer or hang it on a wall as the first plaster cast of a mammal footprint in your collection. To make it more presentable you might colour the footprint to make it stand out a little more.

Dung analysis

Many naturalists make a collection of the dung of British mammals. The dung will contain the undigested portion of the mammal's previous meals and, on examination over a period of days, you can tell what the animal's diet consists of. The way to examine dung is as described below.

Collect the dung and place it in a screw-topped jar for transport home. On arrival home, lift the dung out of the jar and place it on a piece of old nylon stocking. *Note:* Your mother's old nylon stockings are admirably suited to this purpose and can be cut into squares 5in. by 5in. ready for use.

Tie the ends of the piece of nylon together with the dung inside.

Pour warm water into an old enamel basin, gently lower the dung into it and shake it about. Leave it to soak for half an hour or longer.

Remove the nylon bag, open with a needle mounted in a meat skewer and sort over the contents that are left.

You will find wing cases of beetles, bones of small mammals and pieces of vegetation remaining in your nylon bag; these can be identified with practice, then mounted on a card and recorded in your field note-book.

The mammal's home

The set of the badger, earth of the fox or holt of the otter will make an interesting study. To plot their distribution in your own district, to examine each one in turn and to record by means of drawings and notes its location, construction and period of occupation will give you most useful information. Similarly, a squirrel's drey could be examined, and one that is disused could even be brought home and added to your collection. Pull one to pieces to find out the materials used in its construction. List these, and try to trace the source of the materials. This will give you some indication as to whether the squirrel has travelled far in the search of drey materials, or has got them locally. The study of squirrel dreys in a district may reveal peculiarities which are very local. The squirrels may prefer one particular type of tree, or build their dreys always at a certain height. Make notes of these peculiarities and compare your notes with information you can get from naturalists in other areas.

Skulls and bones

Often you will find skulls and bones of animals in the countryside. Friends knowing you are interested may bring them for you to examine. From this material you can add greatly to your collection; skulls are very useful in teaching you the different dental formulae of the families of British mammals (see Appendix E), and the way in which the teeth are adapted to the type of food which they eat.

Skulls can be cleaned by brushing them over with warm water and soap or, if they need more cleaning, by bleaching them in hydrogen peroxide.

Always remember that you should never soak an old skull in water for very long, otherwise the teeth will drop out and the bone will soften and break up.

With skulls or bones of this sort it is useful to write the data on the bone itself with Indian ink, and cover it with gold size. Try to make your printing as small as possible on a part of the bone where it will not be too obvious.

Food signs and storage

Squirrels and a number of mice store food for the winter. Holes in trees or the ground are used as larders to hold the winter store. Gnawed acorns and beech nuts scattered on the ground are sure indications of a hoard in the vicinity. If you examine the food carefully and notice the teeth marks, you will have some idea of the animal which was responsible for collecting or eating them.

The food of our smaller mammals includes acorns, beech nuts, hornbeam nuts, tiny wild cherries, hawthorn seeds, holly seeds, hazel nuts and the cones from certain pine trees. The foods can be collected, identified and mounted on a card with the name of the animal which has either stored them or eaten the kernel from them.

During field activities you will find dead mammals. If you wish, you can make cabinet skins of the bodies for your own private collection.

Making a cabinet skin

The equipment is the same as that you will need for skinning birds and is outlined in Chapter IX.

Preliminary examination
Note down on a piece of paper the exact locality where the mammal was found.

See if you can deduce, from the evidence round about the dead animal, the cause of its death. Details of gunshot wounds or traps should be entered on your card.

Note down the sex of the mammal.

Look for any old scars or damage, particularly to the legs or muscles of the animal.

Make a note of any variation in the colour of its coat or pelt.

Note the colour of the eyes and legs.

Weigh the animal.

Measure the animal. There are five measurements that you can make; they are listed here with details of how to take them.

Head and body measurement: lay the mammal on a flat table on its side. Stretch the body slightly, and place a pin against the animal's nose. Place a second pin or nail pressed right underneath the tail, where the tail bone joins the body. The distance between these two pins is the head and body length, and the measurement should be taken and recorded in millimetres. See diagram below (A [a–b]).

Tail measurement: this is taken from the pin pressed right underneath the tail where the tail bone joins the body, to a second pin pressed against the end of the tail vertebrae, not at the end of the tail fur. Measure the distance in millimetres between these two points and you have the tail measurement. See diagram (D [a–b]).

Total body measurement: this can be obtained by adding

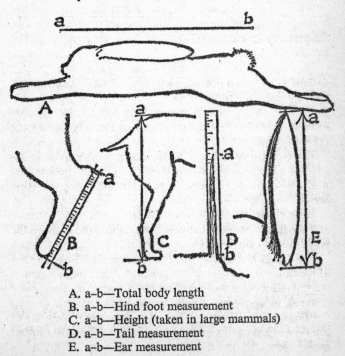

A. a–b—Total body length
B. a–b—Hind foot measurement
C. a–b—Height (taken in large mammals)
D. a–b—Tail measurement
E. a–b—Ear measurement

the head and body length to the tail length; this measurement can be checked by measuring the distance between the pin you placed in position against the animal's nose and the pin placed at the end of the tail vertebrae when the tail was stretched out straight.

Hind foot: this measurement can be taken as illustrated in the diagram (B [a–b]).

Ear measurement: this is taken as in E [a–b] of the diagram.

Skinning
Place the mammal on its back, the tail pointing towards you.

With the point of the scalpel an incision is made in the skin of the stomach from the centre through to the tail.

With the thumb and finger, the skin is loosened from the body at the side of the opening, and by using the fingers and the handle of the scalpel, the skin is loosened as far round to the back as possible.

This exposes the thighs, one of which is drawn up, and by inverting the skin a little, the leg is detached with scissors as close to the body as possible.

Put light magnesium carbonate wherever the blood tends to flow. This absorbs the blood and prevents it from staining the hair of the animal.

The leg is inverted and peeled down to the ankle joint; generally the flesh is now removed from the leg bones – see page 107, para 4. This operation is repeated with the other leg.

The skin round the base of the tail is cut and loosened, and the fingers worked between the skin and the body all the way round to the back to give freedom in stripping the tail.

The tail is inverted as far as it will go. Holding the root of the tail in the fingers of one hand, and the inverted skin of the tail in the fingers of the other hand, by pulling and gently coaxing, using plenty of light magnesium carbonate to keep the fingers from slipping, the tail vertebrae will slip out of the skin or sheath. In mice and squirrels the tail will slip out easily, provided it has not been damaged. With larger

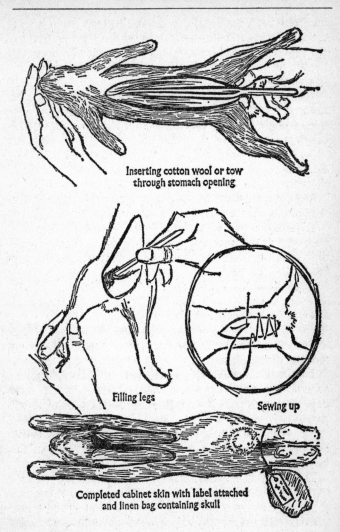

Inserting cotton wool or tow
through stomach opening

Filling legs

Sewing up

Completed cabinet skin with label attached
and linen bag containing skull

mammals you may have to skin along the length of the tail using the scalpel and take the tail vertebrae out by that method. If this is done, the skin must be cleaned and poisoned before the artificial tail is put in and the skin sewn up.

The skin will now peel off easily until the shoulders are reached.

The forelegs are detached close to the shoulders. Continue peeling the skin until the base of the skull is reached.

The ears are severed at the base as close to the skull as possible, and careful skinning beyond the ears will reveal the eyes.

Care is required to avoid cutting the lids of the eyes. Spend time at this point and skin as carefully as you can.

Skinning is continued until the nose is reached. The cartilage is severed at the nose, and the viscera skinned by the roots of the teeth.

With the skin inside out, clean all the meat from the skin. Make sure that all fat has been removed in the region of the leg bones and the tail stump.

Making up the skin
Wrap the cleaned leg bones with cotton wool.

Prepare a wire, wrapped with cotton, to insert in the tail sheath.

Tie the lips to hold the mouth closed. Prepare a length of cotton wool about the length and girth of the natural head and body. Firmly, with forceps, insert into the skin through the stomach opening. Keeping a firm grasp of the forceps, work the skin down upon the cotton wool. Take the cotton wool right up into the head and against the nose, right down to the tail stump.

Still working through the stomach opening, fluff out the cotton wool to fill the skin of the animal.

The end of the bones of the hind legs and the wire projecting from the base of the tail should lie on top of the cotton-wool filling as the animal rests on its back. These are covered with fluffs of cotton wool to prevent them coming in contact with the skin.

Turn the animal over on its stomach, after neatly sewing up the stomach opening and fastening off.

Using the hands, shape and compress the body until it takes the form of the animal's skin illustrated on page 125. Care should be taken not to have the skin too full or bulging. It should be made the same approximate length as the total measurement before skinning. Brush the hair with a brush to remove dust and the light magnesium carbonate, and fasten the skin down on cork, cover with cellophane and place with the label in an airtight cupboard to dry.

Prepare a label to be attached to the rear legs of the specimen cabinet skin. One side of the label should have:

The common and scientific name of the animal.

The locality where the animal was found and the date.

The name of the finder.

Sex.

Whether juvenile or adult.

The second half of the label should have:

The colour of the soft parts of the body.

Preservative used.

Measurements: total head and body lengths, tail length, total body length, ear and hind-limb lengths.

11 REPTILES AND AMPHIBIANS

'Oh, take the horrible thing away!' is the startled remark of a parent when the young naturalist takes an amphibian or reptile home in a jam jar.

Contrary to popular belief, snakes, lizards, toads and frogs are relatively harmless. I say relatively, because there are poisonous snakes. But, if care is taken, no harm can come to the herpetologist or student of these animals.

Even the most elementary knowledge of snakes serves to dispel popular belief, which would have it that mother snake is capable of swallowing her young for protection, or that a snake taking its tail in its mouth forms itself into a hoop and chases its unwary victim, finally killing it with the sting at the end of its tail. These, and many other stories, have grown up about creatures which can be regarded as exciting and novel pets.

Of the six reptiles and six amphibians in this country there is only one that is dangerous. This is the adder (*Vipera berus*), a snake that is recognizable on sight by the black zigzag marking down its back, although it is always as well to remember that snakes vary in their background colour, and it is possible to get a very dark viper where the recognition markings are almost indistinguishable from its scale colour. The head of the adder is somewhat broader than that of the grass snake. This broadness of the head is due to the presence of the enlarged poison glands on either side of it, and is found in an exaggerated degree in many of the deadly poisonous tropical varieties.

In some snakes the poison fangs are connected with the glands by a duct, which, under pressure, delivers the poison in small drops at the root of the fangs. The poison then runs

ADDER

SMOOTH SNAKE

GRASS SNAKE

down the groove in the fang and is thus injected into the wound. In the adder, however, the groove has been closed in the form of a duct which runs down the centre of the tooth and delivers the poison through a hole just above the tip.

It is as well to remember that snakes do not attack or chase you, and that, with few exceptions, the same is true of dangerous snakes in all parts of the world. The snake venom is a modified saliva that helps the snake to digest its food, as well as capture it; digestion of the victim starts even before it is swallowed. The defensive use of the venom is probably secondary.

Until you become an expert with reptiles it is unwise to collect or handle the poisonous kinds. An expert in this case is a man who, over years, has developed a technique and a method from long experience; he is extremely cautious, and never foolhardy where poisonous snakes are concerned.

Collecting equipment

A good strong haversack, preferably leather.

A small flour or sugar bag, with a draw string sewn at the open end.

A forked stick, fashioned from ash or hazel, and rather like the thumb stick used by senior scouts. The forked stick is a very necessary accessory of the snake or reptile collector.

Pond nets.

Plastic bags and screw-topped jars for amphibians and lizards.

Prospecting

Frogs, toads and newts
These can be collected, using a pond net, in most of the ponds and streams in this country.

Lizards and snakes

Warm sunny days are the best times to catch lizards and snakes, particularly in open country away from shade. Should you have any difficulty in locating reptiles and amphibians in your area, the best plan is to ask a local naturalist and he will possibly take you with him on a hunt. When the weather is not warm and sunny, logs, boards and stones form hiding-places for these creatures. Lizards can sometimes be found in old excavations in banks, beneath fallen stone walls and in sand dunes. The young naturalist must be always on the alert so that he can grasp the reptile or amphibian quickly before it recovers from its surprise and shoots away.

Collecting

Frogs, toads and newts

These can be collected either in ponds or streams, or on land in shady, damp places. Care should be taken to see that the specimens are not over-handled, and that when they are put in the jar, plastic bag or cloth flour-bag, there is some damp grass or moss placed inside with them. Immediately after capture, screw down the top of the glass jar, or tie the cloth or plastic bag; otherwise the creatures will escape.

Lizards and snakes

The best time of year for reptile collecting is the spring. Nearly all British reptiles are common at this time, and are found with comparative difficulty later in the year. Next to spring, the early autumn offers the best possibilities for collecting. During hot summers snakes and reptiles seek the shade as a release from the high temperatures, and are often widely scattered.

Weather is a factor to be considered. No collector can expect good results on a day that is rainy or overcast. Reptiles are never found out in inclement weather. The ideal time for collecting is a clear, sunny day towards the end of May or the beginning of June, with no perceptible wind. The temperature should be relatively high in the 60s, and if warm rain has fallen the night before, excellent results may be anticipated.

Having decided on the day for the field trip, the collector should determine what is to be brought along in the way of equipment. For snakes and lizards, linen bags are most suitable. When a reptile is thrust into the bag, it is quickly secured by twisting and tying at the top. A useful piece of collecting equipment is the noose stick, a strong, but slender pole about 5 feet long and moderately tapering towards the end. Driven into the pole at intervals of about 12 inches are a number of small screw-eyes, the last of which is at the very tip of the pole. These screw-eyes are guides for the noose itself, which consists of very fine copper wire. A section about 11 feet long is bent double and both strands of wire threaded through the screw-eyes, starting at the tip of the pole and working towards the part which is to constitute the handle. A loop of wire about 3 inches in diameter should be left protruding from the end of the pole. In manipulating the noose, the pole is held in one hand, the ends of the double wire in the other. When the loop of the wire reaches a point just behind the head of the snake or lizard, the wires are quickly, but gently, pulled tight. The noose is extremely useful for securing lizards which would scamper away very quickly if you were to try and net them, while they do not seem to mind a loop being manoeuvred from a distance over their heads.

Cloth bags should never be overcrowded, nor should they be allowed to remain in the direct rays of the sun for more than a few minutes at a time. Most reptiles are soon overcome by heat.

The young naturalist should develop the habit of overturning all flat rocks and fallen logs that lie in his path on his course of travel through the woods. It is only in this way that the smaller lizards may be found, and, on some occasions, as many as half a dozen snakes may be found under a particularly suitable rock, or on a ledge.

The vivarium

Amphibians and reptiles make attractive and instructive pets if suitably housed in a vivarium. This can be constructed from an old but large box, provided that it is sufficiently large for adequate circulation of air and for visibility, and that there are no rough surfaces. It should be kept in a light airy room, or shed, reached by the rays of the sun for warmth.

The vivarium should have a glass front for viewing, holes at the sides covered with wire gauze for air circulation, and a lid that is removable so that you can examine the specimens and refurnish the plants whenever necessary. With a little ingenuity and elementary carpentry you can construct a very suitable vivarium. Alternatively, an old leaky aquarium would be ideally suitable, provided the top were covered with wire gauze, so that air can circulate freely.

Lay a one-inch layer of dry sand at the bottom of the vivarium. Finely ground fragments of flower pots, or lumps of charcoal, are embedded in the sand for drainage purposes. Over this is laid a half-inch layer of leaf mould. Next, rich garden loam is put in, gradually sloping from a depth of two inches at the back to a depth of half an inch in front. Almost any of the small, low-growing plants one finds in the nearby woods are suitable for transplantation into the vivarium. Ferns always lend a particularly attractive air, as do seedlings of small trees such as spruce or pine or sycamore. The tall plants should be placed in the rear, with the shorter ones growing at the sides and towards the front. At the front, grass seed will provide a suitable growth which should be kept clipped to the desired height. Small lichen – covered rocks, dead bark or a piece of log impart a natural effect. In the front, a saucer of water should be sunk flush with the soil to simulate the small woodland pool.

Once your vivarium is well balanced, it will provide a fascinating study of its inhabitants, surrounded by more or less natural conditions and behaving as they would in the wild state. Lizards frequently will breed under such conditions, giving the young herpetologist the opportunity to record data which is often valuable in filling in blank spaces in the knowledge of the life history of these species.

Handling

A snake that is to be held comfortably needs support. If it is at first active, let it glide about your arms, hands and body at will. If it glides away from your hands, bring one of them up for support under the fore part of the body, and keep moving the hands and arms in this fashion as the snake moves. Usually the snake soon calms down and will rest motionless. Repeated handling will result in a formerly nervous snake becoming completely docile.

Snakes slough the thin outer skin at various intervals. Sometimes this may be only once a year, while if they are feeding regularly it may be as many as three or four times. The skin is shed in one piece if the snake is healthy, and has the opportunity of soaking the entire body in water, thus softening the shed layer. Injured snakes tend to moult more frequently. The moult is started backwards around the snout and the snake, by rubbing against various objects, pulls the skin backwards wrong side out, over the entire length of the body. The snake actually crawls out of the shed layer. Snakes are helped to slough by having some rough bark or rock against which they can rub in the vivarium. Snakes that do not shed properly by themselves should be helped by hand. This failing to slough leads to skin infection and general debilitation.

One sign of the sloughing is that a few days before the moult, the eyes become cloudy, remaining thus for four or five days. During this time, the snakes see only dimly.

Feeding

Snakes will eat frogs, slugs, worms, small fish such as minnows, and insects.

Lizards eat worms, meal worms, slugs and insects.

Preservation

Equipment
    Wide-mouthed, screw-topped glass jars.
    Thin glass.
    Ten per cent formalin.
    Glycerine.
    Gelatine.
    Saucepan and an egg cup.

Reptile mounted on glass and preserved in 10 per cent formalin

Method
The first step is to cut a piece of glass of a suitable size to pass through the wide neck of the glass jar. Next, put a heaped tablespoonful of flaked gelatine in the egg cup and add water until the gelatine is just covered. Allow the mixture to stand for several hours to allow the chemical to absorb the water. Then place the egg cup in the saucepan,

slightly filled with water, and heat over a gas ring until the gelatine melts into a clear liquid. In this condition it is ready for use. Warm the piece of glass, then put a large block of gelatine in the centre and press the reptile's or amphibian's body against this. With more gelatine, and a little dexterity of the fingers, arrange the animal in as natural a position as possible. Write the data on a piece of paper in pencil, and attach it to the lower end of the glass slip with a little of the melted gelatine.

Fill the wide-necked glass jar with 10 per cent formalin, to which 2 or 3 drops of glycerine have been added, then immerse the glass slide in the jar, tightly screw the top and seal with paraffin wax.

Shelled creatures, or to use their technical name, molluscs, are all those animals that have unsegmented bodies, some of which protect themselves with an outer shell or eso-skeleton, composed of calcified material. The mollusca are divided into three sections: the gastropods (from the Greek 'stomach-foot'), including snails, slugs and whelks; the siphonopoda ('tube-foot'), including cuttle fish and squids; and the Pelecypoda ('axe-foot') or lamellibranchiata, which includes mussels, oysters and clams.

Examination of a common garden snail will give an indication of the structure and behaviour of one group of this fascinating family of animals.

If a specimen of a garden snail, or gastropod, is placed in a warm yet damp situation it will emerge from its shell. The long body has a flat base, or sole, from which is secreted a slime to lubricate the snail's path. Except for the sole, the body is rounded and the skin is sensitive to light. The head is furnished with two pairs of 'horns' or tentacles called rhinophores, which are used for feeling and smelling, and which can be pulled in for protection in times of danger. The front pair of tentacles is used in feeling the way; the other two, called ommatophores, are the seeing organs, or eyes, of the snail. The eye, placed at the top of what could be regarded as a conning tower, is a complex instrument, though simpler than our own eyes, and very short-sighted.

The mouth is on the underside of the head, and is furnished with tasting lips and an upper jaw. On the floor of the mouth is a thin horny ribbon of chitin – the tongue, or radula, bearing rows of little curved teeth and looking something like a rasp when magnified. The shape and arrangement of the teeth is constant in every particular species of mollusc. Hence naturalists use the radula as a means of identification when shells look very much alike in their outward structure.

The third class of shells – the pelecypoda – includes mussels, oysters and clams. Here the shell is a bi-valve, that is it is formed in two pieces. Within the two shells lie the organs that are important to the life of the bi-valve. This creature has a mouth, though it has no head, and it does not wander about in search of food, but lies partly embedded in the mud with the shell gaping, waiting for food to come in.

Collecting equipment

Field note-book.

Scoop. The scoop can be constructed from sheet and perforated zinc (see below), either at home or by a metal

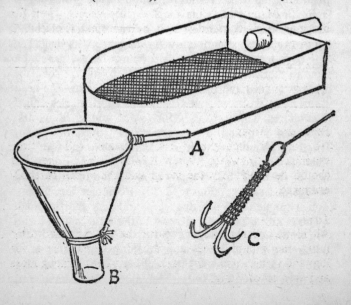

worker. The most suitable shape is the one illustrated, of oblong form with a rounded end, 5in. long, 4in. wide, by 1½in. deep. The bottom is made of perforated zinc, with a ferrule soldered to the back to admit the walking stick.

Walking stick. Used in connexion with the scoop.

Tins and glass tubes. Experience has shown that cardboard pill boxes are unsatisfactory. Not only do certain species of gastropod eat through the board, but the slime and damp condition of the specimen causes disintegration of the pill box. Tins and glass tubes have been found to be by far the best carrying equipment.

Forceps. Used to pick up minute shells.

Cotton wool. Used as padding when packing small shells in collecting tins and tubes. Alternatively, moss can be used.

Old flour bags. Useful for carrying home quantities of leaves and moss for drying and sifting.

Pond net. Made from nylon stocking and fastened on wire frame. Plastic container is detachable (see illustration B on page 138).

Hook. Made from 6-in. nails wired together. Used for dragging weeds on pond or river bottom (see illustration C on page 138).

Where to collect

Ponds and ditches
No pond or ditch should ever be passed without close examination, however barren it may appear. The mud should be sifted with the scoop and the weeds carefully examined.

Land
All moist and shady spots, particularly during and after rain; among dead leaves and decaying vegetation; under logs and stones; under the bark of dead trees; among moss and even on old fungi.

It is important to examine trees as the bark will yield specimens, particularly during summer.

Time to collect

The most suitable collecting times are in early spring, when the animals have just emerged from their winter quarters, and during the autumn, just before they hibernate. Specimens collected during summer should be handled very carefully as certain parts will be newly grown. The most satisfactory collecting time is during, or just after, heavy rain.

Recording

The freshly collected specimens should be carefully packed in a collecting tube or tin, using cotton wool or moss, and the data should be written in pencil on a strip of paper and placed inside. Next, enter full details in the field note-book. These should include:

Exact locality, with map reference.
Date.
Altitude.
Soil details, with notes on immediate environment.

Preservation

Gastropods (*univalves*)
The shells should be cleaned as soon as possible after capture by immersion in boiling water: it is essential that the water is *boiling*, and that the shells are not left in the water for longer than a few seconds.

The animal can be extracted by using a piece of wire or a

hair-pin. For smaller shells a needle is the most suitable instrument.

After the animal has been removed, the shells should be placed in a basin of warm water with the addition of a little soap and carefully washed. With the larger shells, a soft toothbrush can be used to remove mud and give a lustre to the specimen.

Note: the door to the mouth of the shell, technically known as the operculum, can be attached to a plug of cotton wool with glue and placed in position.

Bi-valves

A penknife carefully inserted between the shells will open the bi-valve, after which the animal can be removed easily.

Quickly – speed is essential – thoroughly wash the shells before bringing the two shells together and tying them with a piece of tape. If this is not done, the ligament will harden with the valves open, and, in forcing them shut, the hinge will snap.

Mounting

The most satisfactory method of mounting shells is in glass-topped boxes. These can either be made, or bought from natural-history dealers. There is, however, a great deal of satisfaction in making your own specimen boxes, and they require no great skill, only a little experience.

When the box is made, of a suitable size for the specimens, it should be filled with cotton wool and the specimens neatly laid on top. If the specimens are light coloured, Indian ink can be used to stain the cotton wool black. The specimens will then show to better advantage.

The data should be clearly written in Indian ink on a small slip of paper, which should be placed where it can be seen clearly when the lid is in position.

13 THE SEA-SHORE

The sea-shore is a source of unending pleasure for the young naturalist.

Animals on the shore live in an environment that varies considerably, even with the time of day, as the tide uncovers and covers the shore twice in every 24 hours. Yet, despite these difficult conditions, sea-shore life is abundant both in variety and beauty.

No two stretches of shore are ever alike in their animal population, and if you think of our coast in terms of rocky shore, sandy shore, estuary, sand dunes and mud flats, you will realize what a tremendous opportunity exists for field work.

Precautions are necessary, as many coastal regions can be extremely dangerous at certain times. Buy a time-table from a sports shop, or the local newspaper office, and study it carefully, recording in your field note-book the times of low tide when collecting will be at its best.

Prospect the area carefully, making sure that your collecting area is safe and that you have the opportunity of making a safe retreat if the tide comes in too fast. Often marine biologists get so immersed in their work that they forget there is such a thing as tide until it is nearly too late, and they have to make a run for it to avoid being cut off. This has happened time after time, sometimes with fatal results – so check the nature of the tide or current carefully. One of the best ways of doing this is to chat with a fisherman or coastguard, who will give you all the information you need to know on falling cliffs, tide rise and fall, and currents. Once such people realize how interested you are they will give you a great deal of information on the location of specimens, and even go to the extent of bringing specimens to you.

Comfort is essential on the shore. Rolled-up trousers or a bathing costume help enormously when you are working in a rock pool. A thick cardigan will keep you warm in the cool sea winds. At all times it is essential to wear a pair of old gym shoes as a protection against such things as stinging fish that bury themselves in the sand, sharp stones or broken bottles left behind by thoughtless picnickers.

Collecting equipment

Spade or fork.	Net and handle.
Trowel.	Plastic bottles and screw-
Sieve.	topped containers.
Plastic bucket.	White enamel trays.
	Crowbar.

A small shovel or fork is most useful in collecting on the sea-shore as many small creatures lie buried in the sand and mud and must be dug out. It is useful to pass the damp sand from the low-tide area through a sieve. In this way you will collect a whole host of animals that can be dropped into a screw-topped collecting bottle. Larger creatures are best put into a plastic bucket and covered with sea-water until you have time to sort them over.

A steel crowbar is always useful for turning large stones over and chipping large shellfish from rocks. Shallow white enamel trays are perhaps the most useful item in the sea-shore naturalist's equipment. In these trays you can sort your finds, and they are readily visible against the white enamel.

The net should be made of a strong white cloth, and should be sufficiently small to scrape under stones and into cracks but sufficiently large to capture a good-sized crab.

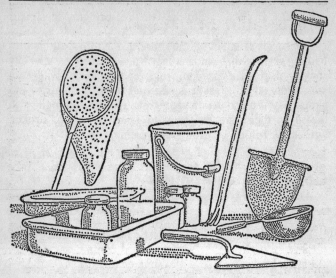

Collecting equipment for the sea-shore

Recording

All finds should be entered in the field note-book with the
following details:

Common name.

Scientific name.

Locality. This will have to be as specific as possible: eg,
'Rock pools 100 yards south of bathing pool and 200
yards north of pier'.

Weather conditions.

State of tide.

Nature of immediate environment from which the specimen was collected: eg, 'Resting against side of rock
pool (Scarborough rock immersed and partially covered
by seaweed)'.

Collector's name.

Date.

Preservation of material

Soft-bodied animals

Soft-bodied animals such as sea anemones, hydroids, sea lemons, sea cucumbers, sea mouse and jelly-fish need to be preserved in a solution of either formalin or alcohol. Formalin can be obtained from a chemist's and is relatively inexpensive. It should be 10 per cent solution of one part of formalin to 10 parts of water with the addition of 10 cc glycerine to prevent the solution hardening the tissues of the animals.

Alcohol is very expensive, particularly in the quantities needed to preserve the larger sea-shore specimens. It can be used for smaller creatures, provided they justify the expense involved.

A good formula that a chemist will make up for you for preserving small but delicate sea creatures is as follows:

	Proportion
Acetic acid (33 per cent)	10 cc
Hydrargyri perchloride (liquid)	10 cc
Glycerine	10 cc
Alcohol (90 per cent)	80 cc
Distilled water	50 cc

The full data should be written in pencil on a slip of paper and attached to the glass so that it is readily visible.

Hard-bodied animals

Hard-bodied animals such as crabs, starfish and chitons can be dried in the sun, or in a drying cupboard.

Starfish and chitons: these should be carefully spread out on boards and tied or wired down. The sooner this is done after they are caught the better, otherwise they will curl up into balls. When they are dry they can be mounted on specially prepared boards, using a good glue, and the data carefully printed beneath.

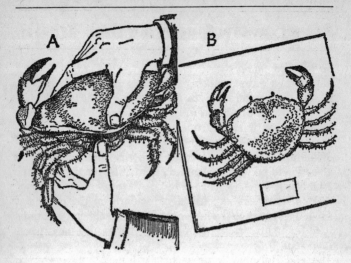

A. Removing carapace of crab
B. Mounted specimen

Crabs: the carapace or shell should be removed and the flesh scraped out. If the specimen is a large one, it may be necessary to remove the legs and clean them thoroughly. All the parts can be stuck together and the crab mounted in a natural position. Thorough cleaning is essential, otherwise you will find mites in your collection.

14 FORMING A NATURE CLUB

A number of enthusiastic young naturalists may wish to join together to form a nature club, society or branch of the British Junior Naturalists' Association. Two things are important in running such a club: the first is that you should have adult guidance, and the second that there should be some form of organization within the club itself.

Guidance

You may say that an adult will spoil the whole thing, and that as a club you can manage perfectly well without a grown person looking after your interests. Now this is not strictly true and you know it. An adult, acting as organizer and chairman of your club or society, can give it tremendous prestige, and help in many ways; by arranging for meeting accommodation, writing on your behalf to landowners when visiting or crossing their land in search of specimens and, above all, by taking the chair at meetings so that the business of the club runs smoothly and efficiently. Although you have an adult organizer for your club, it does not necessarily mean that he is going to make all the decisions, and run the club for you. This is where the organization of the club becomes important, and this aspect is entirely in the hands of yourself, and your young naturalist friends.

Organization

To run your club successfully you must elect the following
officers – a secretary, a treasurer and six serving members. If
it is a mixed club then the girls must take their part in its
administration as well as the boys. In this case it is advisable
that you have three boys and three girls on the committee.
The purpose of the committee is to organize the day-to-day
running of the club, and for this purpose it should meet
regularly in one or other of the committee members' homes.
Many committees I know of make a practice of meeting
once a month. The secretary should inform the members as
to the date and place of the committee meeting, and draw up
an agenda of the business to be discussed at the meeting.
This notice is handed to members well in advance of the
meeting, so that they will have the opportunity to make
suitable arrangements and be able to attend, and that
they are aware as to what will be discussed at the
meeting.

The duties of the committee include:

Arrangement of accommodation for club meetings.

Drawing up a set of rules that are suitable for the members of the club. Rules are important in that they add
prestige to the club and help in the smooth working.

Deciding on a suitable subscription for the club.

Arranging the spring, summer, autumn and winter programmes.

Welcoming new members and seeing that they are made
part of the club or branch they have joined.

Deciding the maximum number of members who should
be allowed to join the club.

Setting an example to all members in the way they should
conduct themselves.

It is important, when electing members on to the committee, that they should be enthusiastic young naturalists
with the interests of the club at heart. A good committee
member is not only a working naturalist, but someone who

is able to make fair decisions and to realize what is in the best interests of the members.

Meetings

Meetings should be held regularly, so that the members know on what day the meeting is being held and at what time, and they will then get into the habit of attending. Many clubs hold their meetings weekly or fortnightly, while some meet only once a month. I feel that a meeting held once a month is not often enough, as members are apt to lose interest. The meetings must be held on a day and at a time that is most convenient to the members of the club. This you will find one of your most difficult problems, as the members will have to fit their club evening among their many other activities. The secretary should draw up the agenda of the meeting and it should take a specific form. The one that is commonly in use I have listed below.

Apologies. The committee should insist that when a member is unable to attend a meeting, he sends his apologies either by a friend, or as a note to the chairman at that meeting.

Minutes. These should be kept by the secretary, who will read them aloud at the meeting. Minutes are important as records, as they will contain observations made by members and information as to what was discussed.

Business arising from the Minutes. This gives the members the opportunity to question anything that happened at the last meeting, and to point out any possible inaccuracies in the minutes.

Any other business. This part of the meeting is left to the chairman and secretary, who may have notices they wish to read out, or points of interest concerning the business of the club that they wish to bring to the notice of members. Such items as overdue subscriptions, visits and future activities can be mentioned at this point. It also gives the members of the club the opportunity to bring up items that they may not be particularly clear about.

Observations and recording. This is a period during the meeting when members can report on the animals and plants they have seen or collected since the last meeting. It is important that these observations should be recorded either in the minutes of the club, or by a recorder – a boy or girl whose job it is to enter them down in a special record book. Observations of this sort are particularly valuable, and should not be allowed to go unrecorded. Members should be encouraged by the committee to bring specimens for exhibition and to stand up and speak about the things they have seen, or the objects they have brought to the meeting. The committee should stress that each report should take no longer than three minutes, otherwise it will be found that this part of the programme takes up far too much time.

Group work. A period of fifteen minutes is set aside for group work, when members who have the same interests can get together in a corner of the room, exchanging ideas and arranging visits for the future. At these meetings the senior boy or girl, with the most experience of his or her subject, can act as group leader, and coordinate the activities of the members of the group towards doing something which will be of value; for instance, the examination of a pond, or a small area of woodland, or perhaps a count of flowers in a pasture. Ecological work of this sort is excellent training in natural history, and it will be found that the different groups can work together in making a survey of this sort, as I shall mention again later in this chapter.

Talk or lecture. The talks should be arranged to cover every aspect of natural history and so satisfy the interests of all the members. Naturalists from the adult societies and local schools will be delighted to come and speak to the club.

The meeting should last for two and a half hours, and as in the typical agenda listed above, it should give everyone the opportunity of taking part in the meeting. After a while you will be surprised at the number of reports you will get: the number of 'finds' which will be brought to the meetings

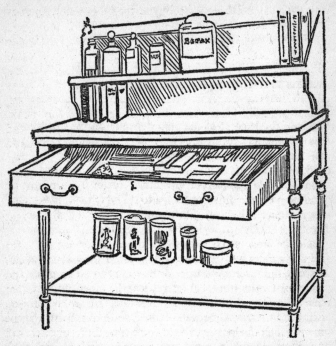

Work table adapted from marble-topped washstand

and the way in which the members take an active part in the group work. The committee should encourage the new members to participate in the proceedings and make sure they do not feel lost and very 'new memberish'.

The guest speaker should be welcomed to the meeting by the chairman or secretary, and be provided with a comfortable chair. He will, as a keen naturalist, be delighted to sit through the meeting and to listen to the observations and reports. It will give him the opportunity of taking back to his own society an excellent report of the club meeting and the club's activities.

The time of meetings is important. You may find that if you hold your meetings on school premises, they will have to be held at 4 PM after school; or, if your organizer gets permission from the local Education Committee to use school premises, they may be held during the early evening.

A programme for the year

Much of the success of the club depends on the attractiveness of the programme. The committee should use its imagination in devising a programme that will meet the needs and interests of all the members, and at the same time stimulate their enthusiasm in natural history. There are a hundred and one different things to do which will make the programme really lively. One committee meeting should be devoted entirely to devising the programme. Programmes should be arranged seasonally, one each for the winter, spring, summer and autumn. A duplicated sheet listing each meeting, the meeting-place and the time should be given to members. Outings of local interest can be arranged, but the committee should bear in mind time and expense. Meetings of this nature should be well planned so that members have time to reach the locality, spend some time there, and return in comfort. If public transport – bus or train – is used, the cost should be kept within the reach of the pocket money of the members, and they should have sufficient warning to be able to put some money aside for the outings.

Below are listed a number of suggestions for each season. These can quite easily be added to, but they will cover the primary needs for most clubs.

Autumn
Bird-watching in small groups, studying migration.

Collection of fungus in woods. Under expert guidance specimens can be identified, edible and poisonous species distinguished, and spore counts made.

Fruits from field and hedgerow can be collected and studied.

Plaster casts can be made of the tracks of animals in soft

mud, looking particularly along the bottom of ditches, the entrance to badger sets and fox earths, and on the banks of rivers for the spoor or 'seal' of the otter.

Owl pellets can be collected, dissected, mounted and the items identified.

Large mammals, such as the badger, can be seen at the set; while small mammals can be observed by using a torch, the light covered with red cellophane.

As the autumn progresses, drawings can be made of the different trees showing the variations in silhouette.

A night walk can be arranged, providing the permission of parents is first obtained. The value of such a walk is that it teaches the members how to use their eyes in the darkness and how to stalk at night, as well as the importance of noise. A walk of this sort could be planned so that members would have the opportunity of visiting badger sets in the vicinity, and possibly of passing a barn or tree where owls are known to be present or active.

Winter
Visiting speakers are important in the winter programme. As I mentioned earlier, members of the adult natural history societies and masters from local schools will be only too pleased to speak to the club. Included in the programme during the winter session might be talks by adults who are youth hostellers, mountaineers, or who have done work outdoors which is of an exciting and adventurous nature.

Making equipment: during the winter months, members can make many items of equipment from material that is readily available. Such items could include pond nets, sweep nets, beating trays, collecting jars, killing bottles and cases to carry their equipment.

Visits to museums: the secretary should make arrangements with the local museum or with agricultural colleges and factories in the district which would be worth visiting during the winter months.

Planning: a number of evenings during the winter programme could be set aside for planning an activity during the spring, summer and autumn of the following year. Work such as an ecological survey of a pond, field, hedgerow or wood would also give the members the opportunity of not only working individually, but also in groups. Each group under its group leader should plan in detail the policy of the work, and the method by which it is going to carry out such things as soil analysis, geological surveys and plant counts.

Films: film strips and films can also be used during the winter. I would stress at this point that films and film strips are aids only, and the club should make every effort to work out its own programme if possible, without resorting to film evenings and quizzes. These can be used as stop gaps, but, wherever possible, the meetings should be so arranged that the members take an active part.

Tracking: interpretation of tracks in snow; these can be plotted and retained as a branch exhibit.

Effect of hard weather on bird life: provision can be made by members for the erection of bird tables.

Spring

Spring migration: members of the club should make observations and records over the spring migratory period. Observations should be kept on the nests in the district. Members can help by seeing that the eggs hatch safely, and that the fledglings leave the nest later.

Bird protection: every year the secretary or the organizer should read out the Protection of Birds Act, 1954, for the benefit of new members to the club. Full details can be obtained from the Royal Society for the Protection of Birds, The Lodge, Sandy, Bedfordshire.

Flowering plants: flowering plants should be collected and mounted on standard sheets or in scrapbooks arranged in families. Identification and mounting should be done in the evenings, using the standard reference keys.

Amphibians: frogs, toads and newts can be studied, and an aquarium set up for members to study the life history of these attractive creatures.

Insects: a start can be made during spring on a reference

collection of Orders of larger insects. Mounting should be done by members of the club, and the collection kept in the club room, where members can make full use of it.

Field note-books and nature diaries: members should be encouraged to keep either a field note-book or a nature diary. A competition can be arranged for the best book at the end of the year. A field note-book differs from a nature diary, in that the field note-book is used only when the boy or girl is out specifically to observe or to collect in the field. The nature diary, on the other hand, is in every sense a diary, kept from day to day, with observations made by the boy or girl while on their way to and from school, while going to the scout or guide meetings and while playing.

Ecological survey: ecological surveys of woodland, pond, pasture or even sea-shore, planned by the group leader during the winter programme, should start as early as possible during the spring. The survey itself should not be conducted on a club evening, but once a month or more often, during the weekend, either on a Saturday or a Sunday. It is a good idea to include the monthly visits in the programme, so that members will know exactly when field work is taking place, what bus to catch and where to meet in the survey area.

Summer

The surveys will be continued throughout the summer and well into the autumn. The interest of the members should not be allowed to flag, and the work on the site should be kept exciting, and new ideas and methods introduced from time to time.

During school holidays, members should organize an expedition for a weekend or a week, preferably to visit an area which will have natural history of a different sort from that in your home town. Camping and hostelling are only two of the many ways in which parties can visit new localities at very little cost.

Members should be encouraged to record, either in note

form or by photographs and drawings, their holiday experiences.

Reptiles: during the summer, the club might keep a vivarium. This can be made either outdoors, in the garden of one of the members, or kept in the club room in an old unused aquarium. Snakes should be kept healthy by including a little dish of water, and by not, of course, having too many snakes in the vivarium at the same time. An evening should be spent by the members studying the difference between the grass snake, the smooth snake and the adder. It is important that members of the club should know how to deal with an adder bite, as well as how the poison mechanism of this snake operates.

Exhibitions: your organizer might make arrangements for the members of your club to hold an exhibition during the summer at one of the meetings of the adult Natural History Society, when the senior members might have the opportunity of seeing the work of club members. At an exhibition of this sort, the more opportunity there is for members to demonstrate the work of the club the better. A member could choose the microscope, demonstrating simple microscopic slides. A second member may show a vivarium or aquarium, stocked with fish, amphibians or reptiles. Mounted herbarium specimens and insects could also be on show. An exhibition of this sort need not necessarily be given only to the adult Natural History Society; it could be open to the public, and possibly a small charge made as an entrance fee to people visiting the exhibition.

Club officers

The hardest-working person in the club will, of course, be the secretary. The boy or girl elected as this officer will have a number of duties, and these will include:

The arrangement of the room for meetings.

The preparation of an agenda for the chairman or organizer.

Recording in a suitable hard-backed book the minutes of the meeting, both at the committee and club meeting.

Reading the minutes at all meetings.

Writing to remind the speaker of the date, time and place of the meeting which he or she will address, and also afterwards writing to thank the speaker for his or her kindness in addressing the club.

Welcoming the speaker to the meeting, and making sure he has a seat, and a cup of tea or some suitable light refreshment afterwards.

Dealing with all the correspondence of the club and, lastly keeping a record of all members.

The treasurer, again a junior naturalist, will have a number of duties, and these will include keeping an up-to-date record of all the subscriptions that are paid by members into the club funds and, at the same time, entering in his book the amount that is spent on items of equipment or oddments that are bought from time to time. He or she will have to present at the annual general meeting a statement of accounts, and these should be brought before the committee before they are presented to the members.

Let the motto of your club be 'Adventure through nature', with lively, active meetings that keep the members enthusiastic.

APPENDIX A

THE BRITISH YOUNG NATURALISTS' ASSOCIATION MERIT AWARD SCHEME

The Merit Award Scheme has been introduced to enable members of the British Young Naturalists' Association to show their proficiency in the field. In each of the five awards the emphasis is on the young naturalists' ability out-of-doors, and to this end the examiner will be an adult field naturalist.

The badges should be worn on the left arm of the jerkin.

Any members of the Association who feel that they have reached the required standard of proficiency can apply to take the Merit Awards by writing to the Natural History Museum, Wood End, The Crescent, Scarborough, when arrangements will be made for the member to be tested in his own area.

Special arrangements can be made for older children who wish to complete the Merit Award Tests.

Special tests are available for handicapped children wishing to qualify.

Junior Naturalist Award

AWARD – FIRST ENAMEL BAR. 10 years

1. Memorize the British Young Naturalists' Association Code.
2. Keep a field note-book and field log for three months.
3. Be able to estimate:
    (a) The height of a tree in the field.

    (b) The wind force.
    (c) The wind direction.
    (d) Magnetic North.

4. Produce carefully mounted and labelled specimens of:
    (a) Six local fossils or rocks.
    (b) Twelve flowering plants.
    (c) Six local ferns or grasses.

5. Produce plaster casts of the spoor of different British mammals.

6. In the field identify:
    (a) Six local birds.
    (b) Six trees by shape, bark or leaves.

7. To demonstrate the use of the public telephone.

Naturalist Award

AWARD – SECOND ENAMEL BAR. 11 years

1. Keep a field note-book and field log for nine months.
2. Be able to read a one-inch Ordnance Survey Map.
3. Give evidence of having studied the wild life of a chosen habitat in your area.
4. Produce carefully mounted and labelled specimens of:
    (a) Six butterflies or moths.
    (b) Six common beetles OR twelve fossils or rocks.
5. Discuss with the examiner the books you would use to identify:
    (a) Wild flowers.
    (b) Birds.
    (c) Mammals.
6. Collect, clean and mount four different shells from two of the following three habitats:
    (a) Freshwater.
    (b) Land.
    (c) Sea-shore.
7. In the field identify:
    (a) Twelve local birds.

    (*b*) Twenty-five wild flowers.

    (*c*) Twelve trees.

Entrants may choose any two out of questions 4, 5 and 6.

Field Naturalist Award

AWARD – Small button-hole badge and THIRD ENAMEL BAR

1. Retake the Young Naturalist Award.

2. Keep a field log for four years.

3. To have produced an interesting summary of local records (where possible).

4. Make a full year's ecological survey of one of the following:
    (*a*) Woodland.
    (*b*) Moor.
    (*c*) Marsh and/or carr.
    (*d*) Shore.
    (*e*) Park.

5. Show familiarity with standard works and identify such specimens as brought by examiner by means of such works.

6. To have made a representative collection of:
    (*a*) British insects.
    (*b*) British fossils.

7. To have watched either:
    (*a*) Badger's set.
    (*b*) Fox's lair.
    (*c*) Otter's holt.
    (*d*) Rabbit's warren.
    (*e*) Mole's fortress.

A definite pattern of behaviour to be shown in notes and diagrams.

8. A dog's or cat's welfare and treatment of a typical injury.

9. Initiative test by branch organizer in cooperation with headquarters.

EIGHT OUT OF NINE QUESTIONS TO BE ATTEMPTED.

Specialist Award

AWARD – CLOTH BADGE. 12 to 13 years

1. Keep a field log for two years and a field note-book for two years.

2. Be able to estimate wind force, temperature and bearings from vegetation.

3. Identify 30 birds by flight, sound or from specimens.

4. Carry out a local survey of birds in one of the following habitats: wood, hedge, moor, park or shore . . . Results to include maps, notes and drawings, photographs if possible, and conclusions to be incorporated in a hard-backed note-book.

5. To be familiar with local, country and national literature on ornithology.

6. Make a cabinet skin.

7. Have a knowledge of bird migration.

SIX OUT OF THE SEVEN QUESTIONS TO BE ATTEMPTED.

The Specialist Award can be taken in any of the following subjects: birds, mammals (including reptiles and amphibians), plants, insects, geology, meteorology, map-making, freshwater biology and marine biology, astronomy artists and forestry. The above is an example for birds.

Diploma

AWARD – METAL STAR AND DIPLOMA. 15 years and upwards

1. To have made a study of ecology of wall, tree, home, fence or one square foot of ground, over a period of at least four months.
2. To show familiarity with a full range of natural-history literature, covering bulletins, journals and local library reference collections.
3. To have carried out suitable group work with not fewer than six children, eg, a survey of a local pond.
4. To show practical knowledge of collecting, preserving and mounting.
5. To produce an original method for the observation and study of a living organism.
6. To have formed a reference collection of British flowering plants, grasses, fungi, mosses and lichens.

FIVE OUT OF THE SIX QUESTIONS TO BE ATTEMPTED.

APPENDIX B

BOOKS TO READ

USEFUL BOOKS ON NATURAL HISTORY

The Young Field Naturalists' Guide by Maxwell Knight (G. Bell).

Field Work in Animal Biology for Young Naturalists by Maxwell Knight (Methuen).

Biology as a Career published by the Institute of Biology.

Dictionary of Biological Terms by I. F. and W. D. Henderson (Oliver and Boyd).

The Standard Natural History, edited by W. P. Pycraft (Warne).

The Penguin Dictionary of British Natural History by Richard Fitter (Penguin and Black).

BOOKS ON MAMMALS

British Mammals by L. H. Matthews (Collins).

Trails, Tracks and Signs by F. J. Speakman (G. Bell).

Living Mammals of the World by I. Sanderson (Hamish Hamilton).

Wild Animals by Keith Shackleton (Nelson).

Handbook of British Mammals edited by H. N. Southern (Blackwell Scientific Publications).

The Mole by Kenneth Mellanby (Collins).

British Wild Animals by R. L. E. Ford (Black).

BOOKS ON BIRDS

Field Guide to the Birds of Britain and Europe by Peterson, Mountford and Hollom (Collins).

The Birds of the British Isles and their Eggs (3 vols) by T. A. Coward (Warne).

Birds of Britain by W. Willett (Black).

How Birds Behave by Neil Ardley (Hamlyn).
Guide to Bird Watching by R. S. R. Fitter (Collins).
Bird Spotting by John Holland (Blandford).

BOOKS ON AMPHIBIANS AND REPTILES
The British Amphibians and Reptiles by Malcolm Smith (Collins).
Lives of British Lizards by Colin Simms (Goose).
British Snakes by L. G. Appleby (John Barker).

BOOKS ON POND AND STREAM LIFE
The Freshwater Life of the British Isles by John Clegg (Warne).
Animal Life in Fresh-Water by H. Mellanby (Methuen).
Life in Lakes and Rivers by T. T. Macan and E. B. Worthington (Collins).
The Observers' Book of Fresh-water Fishes of the British Isles by A. L. Wells (Warne).
Fresh-water Microscopy by W. J. Garnett (Constable).
The Small Water Mammals by Maxwell Knight (Bodley Head).

BOOKS ON MARINE LIFE
The Seashore by C. M. Yonge (Collins).
The Seas by F. S. Russel and C. M. Yonge (Warne).
The Fishes of the British Isles by J. T. Jenkins (Warne).
The Sea Around Us by Rachel Carson (Panther Books).
Seashore (Young Specialist) by A. Kosch, H. Frieling and H. Janus (Burke).

BOOKS ON INSECTS
An Insect Book for the Pocket by Edmund Sandars (Oxford University Press).
Insect Natural History by A. D. Imms (Collins).
The Observers' Book of Common Insects and Spiders by E. F. Linssen and L. H. Newman (Warne).
British Insects by George E. Hyde (Black).
Name This Insect by E. F. Daglish (Dent).

Collecting, Preserving and Studying Insects by H. Oldroyd (Hutchinson).

Grasshoppers, Crickets and Cockroaches of the British Isles by David R. Ragge (Warne).

BOOKS ON BUTTERFLIES AND MOTHS

The Observers' Book of Butterflies by W. J. Stokoe (Warne).

The Observers' Book of the Larger Moths by W. J. Stokoe (Warne).

Know Your Butterflies by C. A. Hall (Black).

BOOKS ON SPIDERS

Spiders by T. H. Savory (Muller).

Spiders and other Arachnids by T. H. Savory (English Universities Press).

BOOKS OF MICROSCOPIC LIFE AND MICROSCOPY

How to Use the Microscope by C. A. Hall and E. F. Linssen (Black).

BOOKS ON ECOLOGY

Woodland Ecology by P. M. Miles and H. B. Miles (Hulton Educational).

Chalkland and Moorland Ecology by P. M. Miles and H. B. Miles (Hulton Educational).

Town Ecology by P. M. Miles and H. B. Miles (Hulton Educational).

Seashore Ecology by P. M. Miles and H. B. Miles (Hulton Educational).

Freshwater Ecology by P. M. Miles and H. B. Miles (Hulton Educational).

Practical Field Ecology by R. C. McLean and W. R. I. Cook (Allen and Unwin).

Woodland Ecology by E. G. Neal (Heinemann).

BOOKS ON FLOWERS

Wild Flowers by John Gilmour and Max Walters (Collins).

Guide to Wild Flowers by David McClintock and R. S. R. Fitter (Collins).

Wayside and Woodland Blossoms (3 vols) by E. Step (Warne).
The Observers' Book of Wild Flowers by W. J. Stokoe (Warne).
Wild Flowers by W. R. Philipson (Black).
Flora of the British Isles by Clapham, Tutin and Warburg (Cambridge University Press).

BOOKS ON TREES
Trees and Bushes in Wood and Hedgerow by H. Vedel and Johan Lange (Methuen).
Guide to British Hardwoods by W. B. R. Laidlaw (Leonard Hill).
Know Your Broadleaves – Forestry Commission Booklet No 20 (HMSO).
Know Your Conifers – Forestry Commission Booklet No 15 (HMSO).

BOOKS ON FERNS AND MOSSES
Wayside and Woodland Ferns by E. Step (Warne).
The Observers' Book of Mosses and Liverworts by A. L. Jewell (Warne).
The Observers' Book of Ferns by W. J. Stokoe (Warne).

BOOKS ON FUNGI
The Observers' Book of Common Fungi by E. M. Wakefield (Warne).
Mushrooms and Toadstools by John Ramsbottom (Collins).
Introduction to Mycology by J. A. MacDonald (Butterworth).

BOOKS ON ALGAE
Seaweeds and their Uses by V. J. Chapman (Methuen).

BOOKS ON FOSSILS, ROCKS AND MINERALS
Rutley's Elements of Mineralogy, revised by H. H. Read (Murby).
The Pebbles on the Beach by C. Ellis (Faber and Faber).
Minerals and how to Study Them by E. S. Dana (Chapman and Hall).

Study of Rocks by S. J. Shand (Allen and Unwin).
Life before Man: the Story of Fossils by D. Forbes (Black).
A Guide to Earth History by Richard Carrington (Chatto and Windus).

BOOKS ON CLIMATE AND WEATHER
Climate and the British Scene by Gordon Manley (Collins).
Shore Life, Fishes, Clouds and Weather by H. Trevor Jones (Warne).
Climate through the Ages by C. E. P. Brooks (Benn).
Teach Yourself Meteorology by Aeouls (English Universities Press).

APPENDIX C

NATURAL HISTORY ORGANIZATIONS

ANIMAL PROTECTION

Royal Society for the Prevention of Cruelty to Animals, 105 Jermyn Street, London, SW1.

   Publication: *Animal World* (monthly).

Fauna Preservation Society, Zoological Gardens, Regent's Park, London, NW1.

   Publication: *Oryx* (quarterly).

The Royal Society for the Protection of Birds, The Lodge, Sandy, Bedfordshire.

   Publication: *Bird Notes* (quarterly).

JUNIOR NATURAL HISTORY

British Young Naturalists' Association, c/o Natural History Museum, Wood End, Scarborough.

   Publication: *The Young Naturalist* (monthly).

ENTOMOLOGICAL

The Amateur Entomologists' Society, 54 Gyles Park, Stanmore, Middlesex.

   Publication: *Bulletin* (11 published each year).

Royal Entomological Society of London, 41 Queen's Gate, South Kensington, London, SW7.

   Publications:
   Series of Keys for the Identification of British Insects.
   Proceedings and Transactions.

BOTANICAL

Botanical Society of the British Isles, Peniston Road, London, SW16.

Publications:
Watsonia (three parts each year).
Year Book (annually).
British Mycological Society, Dept of Botany, The University, Southampton.

BIRDS

British Trust for Ornithology, 2 King Edward Street, Oxford.
Publications:
Annual Report
Bird Study (quarterly magazine).
Miscellaneous publications of value to field ornithologists, including Field Guide No 2 – *How to Choose Binoculars*.

British Ornithologists' Union, London Zoo, Regent's Park, London, NW1.
Publications: *Ibis* (quarterly journal).

MAMMALS

The Mammal Society, c/o Dept of Extra Mural Studies, University of Birmingham, Edmund Street, Birmingham, 3.

SHELLS

Conchological Society of Great Britain and Ireland, The Nook, Uplands, Bromborough, Cheshire.
Publication: *Journal of Conchology* (twice yearly).

GEOLOGY

Geological Society of London, Burlington House, Piccadilly, London, W1.
Publications:
Journal (quarterly).
Proceedings (abstracts).
The Geologists' Association, Geological Survey and Museum, Exhibition Road, London, SW7.
Publication: *Proceedings*.

The Mineralogical Society of Great Britain and Ireland, 41 Queen's Gate, London, SW7.

Publications: *Mineralogical Magazine and Journal of the Society.*

GENERAL

Council for Nature, Zoological Gardens, Regent's Park, London, NW1.

Publications:

News for Naturalists.

Monthly Press Bulletin.

School Nature Study Union, 12 Cranes Park Avenue, Surbiton, Surrey.

Publications: *School Nature Study* (quarterly).

Freshwater Biological Association, The Ferry House, Far Sawrey, Ambleside, Westmorland.

Publication: *Animal Report.*

Marine Biological Association of the United Kingdom, The Laboratory, Citadel Hill, Plymouth.

Publications: *Journal of the Marine Biological Association.*

Zoological Society of London, Regent's Park, London, NW1.

Publications:

Proceedings (quarterly).

Transactions (irregular intervals).

Royal Microscopical Society, BMA House, Tavistock Square, London.

Publication: *Journal* (quarterly).

London Natural History Society, London School of Hygiene and Tropical Medicine, Keppel Street (Gower Street), London, WC1.

Publications:

The London Naturalist (annually).

London Bird Report (annually).

Museums Association, 87 Charlotte Street, London, W1.

Publication: *Museums Journal* (monthly).

Each county has a Natural History Organization and these normally publish a quarterly transaction or journal.

Full details can be obtained from:

Directory of Natural History and Field Study Societies, Great Britain and Ireland. (Published by the British Association for the Advancement of Science.)

APPENDIX D

FIELD STUDY CENTRES AND BIRD OBSERVATORIES

THE BRITISH YOUNG NATURALISTS' ASSOCIATION
Field Study Centre and Trailside Museum, 'The Holt'.
  Hutton Buscel, near Scarborough.

Residential courses for young naturalists, with expert tutors, during the Easter and August holidays.

The Centre is available for hire during term time. All inquiries regarding bookings should be addressed to: The Natural History Museum, Wood End, The Crescent, Scarborough.

YORKSHIRE FIELD STUDIES
Residential field courses for young naturalists are organized during school holidays. The courses cover natural history, geology, forestry, archaeology, history, sea-shore studies and geography. All inquiries regarding bookings should be addressed to: The Director, Yorkshire Field Studies, Larpool Hall, Whitby, Yorks.

FIELD CENTRES
English
Flatford Mill Field Centre, near Colchester, Essex.
Juniper Hall Field Centre, near Dorking, Surrey.
Malham Tarn Field Centre, near Settle, Yorks.
Dale Fort Field Centre, near Haverfordwest, Pembrokeshire.
Preston Montford Field Centre, near Shrewsbury, Salop.
Slapton Ley Field Centre, South Devon.

Scottish
Garth Field Studies Centre, by Aberfeldy, Perthshire.

BIRD OBSERVATORIES

Fair Isle Bird Observatory, Lerwick, Scotland.
Warden: P. E. Davis.
Accommodation for 14 visitors.

Isle of May Bird Observatory and Field Station, Fife.
Accommodation for 6 visitors.
Visitors must bring own food, including milk and eggs.

Spurn Bird Observatory, Warren Cottage, Kilnsea, Yorks.
Administered by a special committee of the YNU.
Hon Sec: G. H. Ainsworth, 144 Gillshill Road, Hull, who
is in charge of bookings.
Visitors bringing their own sheets and pillowcases.

Gibraltar Point Bird Observatory and Field Study Centre,
near Skegness, Lincs.
Administered by the Lincolnshire Naturalists' Trust.
Hon Sec: A. E. Smith, Pyewipes, Willoughby, Alford,
Lincs.
Limited accommodation at the observatory.

Cley Bird Observatory, Holt, Norfolk.
Warden: R. A. Richardson, Hilltop, Cley.
Limited accommodation at the observatory for those with
ringing experience only.

Bardsey Bird and Field Observatory, Aberdaron, North
Wales.
Warden: R. W. Arthur.
Accommodation for 8 visitors.

The New Grounds, Slimbridge, Glos. (Headquarters of the
Wildfowl Trust).
Director: Peter Scott.
Accommodation: No hostel accommodation is available at
present, but a list of places to stay nearby is available
from the Bookings Secretary.

Skokholm Bird Observatory, Dale, Haverfordwest, Pembs.
Warden: Mrs Kate Barham.
Accommodation: 8–10 visitors.

Lundy Field Station and Observatory, *via* Bideford, Devon.
Warden: W. B. Workman.
Accommodation: 10 visitors, who must be members of the
    Lundy Field Society.

Dungeness Bird Observatory, Romney Marsh, Kent.
Accommodation for up to 12 visitors.

Jersey Bird Observatory, St Ouen's Nature Reserve, Jersey.
Accommodation arranged locally.

Portland Bird Observatory, Portland, Dorset.
Accommodation: 6 visitors.

Copeland Bird Observatory, Northern Ireland.
Director: J. G. Gray, 24 Aigburgh Park, Belfast.
Hon Sec: G. T. Flock, 27 Hillside Road, Stranmillis, Belfast,
    from whom further details can be obtained.

The Saltee Bird Observatory, Co Wexford, Ireland.
Accommodation: 4–6 visitors.

APPENDIX E

MUSEUMS IN GREAT BRITAIN WHICH EXHIBIT NATURAL HISTORY SPECIMENS

ABERDEEN
Natural History Museum, Marischal College, University of Aberdeen.

AYLESBURY
County Museum, Church Street, Aylesbury.

BARNSLEY
The Museum, Harvey Institute, Eldon Street, Barnsley.

BELFAST
Museum and Art Gallery, Stranmillis, Belfast.

BIRMINGHAM
City Museum and Art Gallery, Congreve Street, Birmingham.

BOLTON
Museum and Art Gallery, Civic Centre, Bolton.

BRADFORD
City Art Gallery and Museum, Cartwright Memorial Hall, Bradford 9.

BRISTOL
City Museum, Queen's Road, Bristol 8.

CARDIFF
The National Museum of Wales, Cathays Park, Cardiff.

CARLISLE
Museum and Art Gallery, Tullie House, Carlisle.

COLCHESTER
Colchester and Essex Museum, The Castle, Colchester.

COVENTRY
City Museum and Herbert Temporary Art Gallery, Coventry.

DONCASTER
Museum and Art Gallery, Waterdale, Doncaster.

DUBLIN
National Museum of Ireland, Kildare Street, Dublin.

DUNDEE
Central Museum and Fine Art Gallery, Albert Institute, Dundee.

EDINBURGH
The Royal Scottish Museum, Chambers Street, Edinburgh.

EXETER
Royal Albert Memorial Museum, Queen Street, Exeter.

GLASGOW
Art Gallery and Museum, Kelvingrove, Glasgow, C3.

GLOUCESTER
City Museum, Brunswick Road, Gloucester.

HALIFAX
Bankfield Museum, Ackroyd Park, Halifax.

HASLEMERE
The Educational Museum, High Street, Haslemere.

HUDDERSFIELD
Tolson Memorial Museum, Ravensknowle Park, Huddersfield.

IPSWICH
Museum of Natural History, High Street, Ipswich.

LEEDS
City Museum, Park Row, Leeds 1.

LEICESTER
Museum and Art Gallery, New Walk, Leicester.

LINCOLN
City and County Museum, Broadgate, Lincoln.

LIVERPOOL
Public Museum, William Brown Street, Liverpool.

LONDON
British Museum of Natural History, Cromwell Road, London, SW7.

LUTON
Museum and Art Gallery, Wardown Park, Luton.

MAIDSTONE
Museum and Art Gallery, St Faith Street, Maidstone.
MANCHESTER
City Art Gallery and Museum, Mosley Street, Manchester 2.
NEWCASTLE ON TYNE
Hancock Museum, Barras Bridge, Newcastle on Tyne 2.
NORTHAMPTON
Central Museum and Art Gallery, Guildhall Road,
    Northampton.
NORWICH
Castle Museum, Castle Meadow, Norwich.
NOTTINGHAM
Natural History Museum, Wollaton Park, Nottingham.
PLYMOUTH
City Museum and Art Gallery, Tavistock Road, Plymouth.
READING
Museum and Art Gallery, Blagrave Street, Reading.
ROTHESAY
The Bute Museum, Stuart Street, Rothesay.
SCARBOROUGH
Museum of Natural History, Wood End, The Crescent,
    Scarborough.
SHEFFIELD
City Museum, Weston Park, Sheffield 10.
STOKE ON TRENT
City Museums and Art Gallery, Broad Street, Hanley,
    Stoke on Trent.
WARWICK
County Museum, Market Place, Warwick.
YORK
Philosophical Museum, York.

APPENDIX F

NATURAL HISTORY DEALERS

ANIMAL SUPPLIERS

Falsgrave Pet Stores, 48 Falsgrave Road, Scarborough.
Birds, animals, fish, reptiles. Suppliers of cages.

Thearne Pet Stores, 32 West Street, Hull.
Birds, animals, fish. Suppliers of cages.

Tysely Pet Stores, 771 Warwick Road, Birmingham 11.
Birds, animals.

Robert Jackson, Ltd, Holly Bank Nurseries, Grove Lane, Hale, Cheshire.
Animals, reptiles.

Keston Foreign Bird Farm, Brambletye, Keston, Kent.
Foreign birds.

Shirley Aquatics Ltd, Stratford Road, Monkspath, Shirley, Warwickshire.
Tropical fish.

Tachbrook Tropicals, 244 Vauxhall Bridge Road, London.
Tropical fish.

OUTDOOR SUPPLIES

Adventure Supplies, 1 York Place, Scarborough.
All collecting equipment, walking, camping, cycling and underwater swimming supplies.

Broadhurst Clarkson & Co Ltd, 63 Farringdon Road, London, EC1.
Binoculars and telescopes.

Wallace Heaton, 127 New Bond Street, London, W1.
Binoculars.

ENTOMOLOGICAL SUPPLIES

L. Christie, 137 Gleneldon Road, Streatham, London, SW7.

L. Hugh Newman, FRES, FRHS, The Butterfly Farm, 41–2 Salisbury Road, Bexley, Kent.

T. J. Honeybourne, FRES, FRHS, 'Laceys', 97 Birchwood Road, Wilmington, Dartford, Kent.

BIOLOGICAL AND NATURAL HISTORY SUPPLIES

Watkins and Doncaster, 110 Park View Road, Welling, Kent.
All types of natural history equipment.

Flatters and Garnett Ltd, 309 Oxford Road, Manchester 13.
General biological supplies.

P. K. Dutt and Co Ltd, 1–2 Alfred Place, Store Street, London, WC1.

APPENDIX G

NATURAL HISTORY MAGAZINES

Entomologist (monthly)
Dr E. Popham, Dept of Zoology, Manchester University,
   Manchester.

Entomologists' Monthly Magazine
Nathaniel Lloyd and Co Ltd, Burrell Street Works, Black-
   friars, London, SE1.

Entomological Gazette
E. W. Carsey, 22 Harlington Road, East Feltham, Middlesex.

British Birds (monthly)
H. F. and G. Witherby, 5 Warwick Court, Holborn, London,
   WC1.

Annals and Magazine Natural History (monthly)
Taylor and Francis Ltd, 18 Red Lion Court, London, EC4.

Young Naturalist (monthly)
The Dalesman Publishing Company, Clapham, *via* Lancaster.

Piccolo General

Piccolo Fiction

Puzzles and Games